Natural Settings

Natural Settings

Creating Botanical Jewelry
with Eco-resins

Sharon Wu

HERBERT PRESS

LONDON · OXFORD · NEW YORK · NEW DELHI · SYDNEY

HERBERT PRESS
Bloomsbury Publishing Plc
50 Bedford Square, London, WC1B 3DP, UK
Bloomsbury Publishing Ireland Limited,
29 Earlsfort Terrace, Dublin 2, D02 AY28, Ireland

BLOOMSBURY, HERBERT PRESS and the Herbert Press logo are
trademarks of Bloomsbury Publishing Plc

First published in Great Britain 2026

A catalogue record for this book is available from the British Library
Library of Congress Cataloguing-in-Publication data has been applied
for

ISBN: 978-1-78994-345-0; eBook: 978-1-78994-346-7

2 4 6 8 10 9 7 5 3 1

Page layout design by Jerry Goldie Graphic Design
Printed and bound in China by RR Donnelley Asia Printing Solutions Ltd

To find out more about our authors and books visit www.bloomsbury.
com and sign up for our newsletters
For product safety related questions contact productsafety@
bloomsbury.com

To my mom

For opening my eyes to the wonder in

every leaf and flower

Contents

The Projects

Project 1:
Whole marigold earrings

Project 6:
Purple primrose earrings

Project 10:
Pink bougainvillea earrings

Project 2:
Half marigold earrings

Project 7:
Red maple necklace

Project 11:
Purple hydrangea frame earrings

Project 3:
Fig earrings

Project 8:
Blue hydrangea bracelet

Project 12:
Hydrangea multiple flower earrings

Project 4:
White hydrangea pearl earrings

Project 9:
White and purple viola earrings

Project 13:
Fleabane daisy earrings

Project 5:
Pink marble carnation earrings

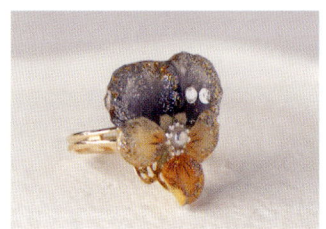

Project 9 variation:
Orange and purple viola ring

Project 14:
Purple lantana necklace

Project 15:
Purple statice, blue cornflower, and orange marigold earrings

Project 19 variation:
Round fall leaf earrings

Project 24:
Blue cornflower earrings

Project 29:
Rice flower earrings

Project 16:
Purple statice and blue cornflower necklace

Project 20:
Rabbit ear grass earrings

Project 25:
Acorn necklace

Project 30:
Purple and white baby's breath pendant

Project 17:
Purple and orange viola earrings

Project 21:
Forget-me-not necklace

Project 26:
Forget-me-not earrings

Project 31:
Cypress earrings

Project 18:
Blue lobelia earrings

Project 22:
Purple verbena earrings

Project 27:
White daisy earrings

Project 32:
Purple statice and blue cornflower large earrings

Project 19:
Oval fall leaf earrings

Project 23:
Rose petal necklace

Project 28:
Blue and green baby's breath earrings

Project 33:
Christmas earrings

Introduction

Resin botanical jewelry is a unique blend of nature and art, allowing crafters to capture nature's magnificent beauty and unique memories. This book serves as a comprehensive guide, covering everything from understanding the fundamentals of resin to mastering advanced resin flower jewelry-making techniques. It is designed to empower you with the knowledge and skills you will need to craft stunning and sustainable resin jewelry.

A perfect blend of nature and art

Nature has an effortless beauty, and resin allows us to preserve and enhance it in a way that feels both magical and timeless.

Preserving nature's beauty

Encasing flowers in resin isn't just about making jewelry; it's about capturing a fleeting moment in time. Delicate petals, leaves, and even tiny seeds are frozen in their prime, their details forever preserved. The crystal-clear resin highlights every nuance – the soft curves of a petal, the intricate veins of a leaf – making it feel as if nature is still alive within the piece.

Enhancing natural elegance

Resin amplifies the beauty of botanical elements, making colors richer and textures more defined. Its glossy surface acts like a magnifying glass, bringing out the vibrancy of each inclusion. The smooth, domed finish intensifies the colors and details, giving nature an extra touch of brilliance.

The perfect harmony of organic and engineered

The fusion of raw natural beauty with precise craftsmanship results in jewelry that is both timeless and one-of-a-kind:

Organic fluidity: The natural irregularity of flowers and leaves adds a sense of movement and spontaneity.

Top: **Flowers set in resin, ready for finishing.**
Above: **Flower resin cabochon under curing.**
Left: **A trio of botanical resin earrings.**

Engineered precision: Resin provides structure, durability, and a flawless finish, offering a modern contrast to nature's unpredictability.

Adding depth and dimension

Layering is where the magic happens. By combining multiple flowers, adding subtle hints of glitter, or experimenting with tinted resins, you can create a mesmerizing sense of depth. Each layer builds upon the last, forming a miniature world of nature inside your piece.

More than just jewelry, resin botanical creations are tiny keepsakes – snapshots of special moments, favorite blooms, or personal symbols. Every piece tells a story, holding a piece of nature and a part of your heart.

Left: **Botanical elements encapsulated in resin using molds in various shapes.**

Above: **Various designs with the same mold.**

Right: **Cured and demolded botanical resin pieces.**

Natural vs. petroleum-based resins

At the heart of this book is a deep appreciation for the beauty of nature – and a commitment to protecting it. That's why every project featured here uses natural-source resins. For me, this isn't just a creative choice, it's the soul of the book. Unlike traditional craft resins derived from petroleum, natural plant-based resins offer a far more eco-conscious alternative, making them the perfect fit for artists who care about the planet as much as their craft.

Natural resins are derived from renewable sources – plants, trees, and other biological materials – rather than fossil fuels. They carry a significantly lower environmental impact across their lifecycle, and are often less toxic, with some being biodegradable. Using them means reducing our reliance on non-renewable resources and limiting exposure to harmful chemicals, both for ourselves and for the Earth.

Like any material, plant-based resins are not without limitations, and these challenges will be discussed more in the following section. For most hobbyists and nature-inspired makers, the trade-offs are minor – especially when weighed against the environmental benefits and the satisfaction of using sustainable materials. Many crafters find that working with natural resins feels more harmonious, more intentional and more connected to the organic beauty we're preserving in our jewelry.

In the later chapters, we'll explore different types of natural resins and how to work with them effectively, without needing a science degree!

But, for now, just know that choosing natural resins is a creative decision that aligns your art with your values.

Advantages of using plant-based resins

1. **Renewable resources:** The use of plant-derived ingredients minimizes reliance on non-renewable resources, promoting sustainability.
2. **Lower carbon footprint:** Plant-based resins generate fewer greenhouse gas emissions during production, aligning with eco-conscious practices.
3. **Biodegradability:** Some plant-based resins decompose more readily in natural environments, reducing waste accumulation. Plant-based epoxy resins and UV resins on the market are usually not biodegradable.

4. **Less toxic options:** Many plant-based resins are formulated to be free from or contain fewer harmful chemicals, making them safer for users and the environment. However, keep in mind that some plant-based resins may still contain some harmful chemicals and require proper safety precautions during use. Ventilation and protective equipment (gloves and masks) are still necessary when working with these resins.

Of course, natural resins come with their own set of characteristics. They may cure more slowly or be slightly more sensitive to humidity or UV exposure compared to their petroleum-based counterparts. They may also have a slightly shorter shelf life or different working properties.

Disadvantages of using plant-based resins

1. **Limited availability:** Plant-based resins are not as widely available as traditional options, potentially making them harder to source. In my projects I use green epoxy with over 60 percent plant based ingredients and plant-based UV resin for 3D printing.

2. **Higher cost:** The production of plant-based resins can cost at least 50 percent more than traditional resins.

3. **Performance variability:** While advances continue to be made, some plant-based resins may not yet match the durability or clarity of their fossil-fuel-based counterparts. Plant-based resins often exhibit a hint of yellow compared to conventional resins.

Right: **Earrings made with plant-based resins: two-component epoxy resin and UV resin.**

4. **Processing challenges:** Plant-based resins may require specific conditions or additives to achieve optimal curing and strength, complicating the crafting process for beginners.

Plant-based epoxy craft resins are readily available online from brands like EcoPoxy and Nerpa (see Suppliers on p.172). Plant-based UV resins also exist, though they are primarily designed for 3D printing (e.g., Anycubic and Elegoo plant-based UV resins). These resins can be cured under standard UV light, but the process takes longer unless specialized equipment is used.

I use a SLA (stereolithography) 3D printer – a process that uses a UV laser to cure liquid resin layer by layer – and its accompanying UV chamber, which speeds up curing. The resin used in SLA printing is a liquid photopolymer that solidifies when exposed to UV light. This UV resin comes in various formulations, including standard, flexible, tough, and castable types, depending on the application's needs.

Plant-based (vegan and cruelty-free) gel nail polishes are also incorporated in some projects and

Table 1: Regular UV vs. plant-based UV resin for jewelry making

	Regular UV resin	Plant-based UV resin
Eco-friendliness	Petroleum-based	Plant-based
Viscosity	Low, medium, and high	Low viscosity. However, plant-based nail gel can be used for medium- and high-viscosity UV resin
Curing time	1–3 minutes	2–6 minutes
Odor and Volatile Organic Compounds (VOCs)	Varies by brand; some art resins have low odor	Lower odor; fewer VOCs
Clarity and gloss	High gloss	High gloss, some variations between brands
Safety	Can release fumes	Safer, less toxic formulas

Table 2: Processability and property comparison between epoxy and UV resin

	Processability	Resin properties
Epoxy resin	Pros: Self-leveling: Ensures a smooth surface without much effort. Long working time: Allows ample time to remove bubbles and adjust designs. Versatile: Can be mixed with pigments, glitter, and inclusions like flowers or beads. Cons: Mixing required: Two-component system, requiring additional measuring and mixing tools. Sticky residue: Improper mixing can result in sticky or uneven surfaces. Health concerns: Emits fumes during curing; requires good ventilation and safety gear. Slow curing time: Takes 24–72 hours to fully cure.	Pros: Scratch resistant: Glossy and transparent surface. Opaque: Allows designs with high loading of pigments and decorative fillers. Cons: Prone to yellowing: It also can soften under prolonged heat or sunlight.
UV resin	Pros: Simple process: No need to mix components; ready to use directly. Unlimited working time: Stays liquid until exposed to UV light. Quick curing: Cures in minutes under a UV light. Allows multilayer building in a short period of time. Low health concerns: Zero to very low VOC and toxic ingredients. Cons: Higher cost: More expensive than epoxy resin. Requires UV light: Additional equipment is necessary for curing. Mismatch of wavelength or not enough light exposure can lead to sticky surface.	Pros: High gloss or matte finish possible: Results in a shiny, glass-like surface. Cons: Limited loading level: Though opaque design is possible, loading levels of fillers and pigments are limited.

Note: Volatile organic compound (VOC) refers to a class of organic chemicals that easily evaporate into the air at room temperature. VOCs can cause serious health effects.

are widely available through a simple online search.

For jewelry making, I prefer UV resin over epoxy resin because of its faster processing time. Accordingly, most projects in this book feature UV resin. However, for bulk production, epoxy resin is a more economical choice.

Artists can choose their preferred resin type. Different regions offer various brands and formulations of epoxy and UV resin. Researching local options with low odor and high UV resistance is recommended for the best results.

Desired properties of resins for resin flower jewelry

Processability

1. **Handling:** Ideally requires no mixing or simple mixing. The curing process is insensitive to humidity and temperature.
2. **Viscosity:** The thickness of the resin determines its suitability for different techniques, such as layering or casting.
3. **Pot life:** The longer the pot life the better. As dried flowers are delicate, you will and need to work slowly.
4. **Cure time:** The shorter the cure time the better, as many projects require layer-by-layer build up.
5. **Low VOC and toxicity:** Low VOC and toxicity of the uncured resin.

Cured property

1. **Clarity:** High-quality resins offer crystal-clear finishes, essential for jewelry that highlights embedded items.

2. **Moisture resistance:** Resins exhibit strong resistance to humidity, water and mold.
3. **Durability:** Resins are known for their strength and resistance to wear.
4. **UV resistance:** UV-stabilized resins prevent yellowing and degradation when exposed to sunlight.

Based on these requirements, plant-based polyester and polyurethane resins are not as well suited to jewelry making as plant-based UV and epoxy resins. This is due to shorter pot life (typically less than 10 minutes), the need for more precise mixing, higher levels of VOC, higher toxicity monomers (styrene and isocyanate), and sensitivity to moisture.

Above: **Silicone molds allow me to layer, shape, and preserve intricate details, turning natural elements into three-dimensional creations with a flawless finish**

Right: **UV resin encapsulated Queen Anne's lace flower in a golden heart pendant.**

Resin Crafting 101

The first and most important step of learning resin craft is to understand how to use resin safely. Whether you're making a simple pendant or more complex designs, knowing resin types, properties, and applications will enhance your experience. By adhering to the following guidelines, you can enjoy working with resin while minimizing health risks.

Tips for working safely with resin

Using personal protective equipment (PPE)

When working with resin, you will need to protect yourself by wearing the following PPE:

- **Gloves:** Always use nitrile gloves when working with epoxy resin to avoid skin contact, as it can cause irritation or allergic reactions. Wearing gloves is also recommended when working with UV resin, if you have sensitive skin. As you become more skilled, you can work without gloves but always be prepared with wet wipes at hand.
- **Eye protection:** Use safety goggles with side coverings to protect against splashes.
- **Respirator mask:** If you need to work with epoxy resin in large amounts or for a long period of time, or if you are very sensitive to fumes and VOCs, wear a respirator with organic vapor cartridges. When sanding the resin, wear a fine filter mask.
- **Protective clothing:** Wear long sleeves or aprons to prevent resin from soaking into your skin or clothing.

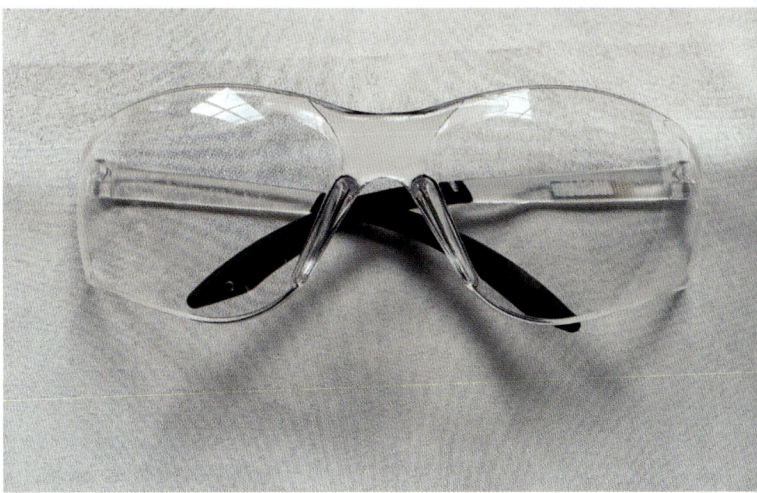

Left: **UV resin coated bluebonnet flowers under curing.**

Right: **The two essential items of PPE: gloves and eye protection.**

Preparing your working area

Work in a well-lit, clean, flat, and uncluttered dedicated area to prevent accidental spills and to make any cleanups easier:

- Make sure your workspace is well ventilated – a table next to an open window is an easy set up. Ensure proper airflow by opening windows or setting up exhaust fans to pull fumes away from your workspace.
- Use wax paper or reusable silicone mats to cover your work area for easy cleanup.
- Regularly clean mats with wipes and packing tape to remove resin residue.

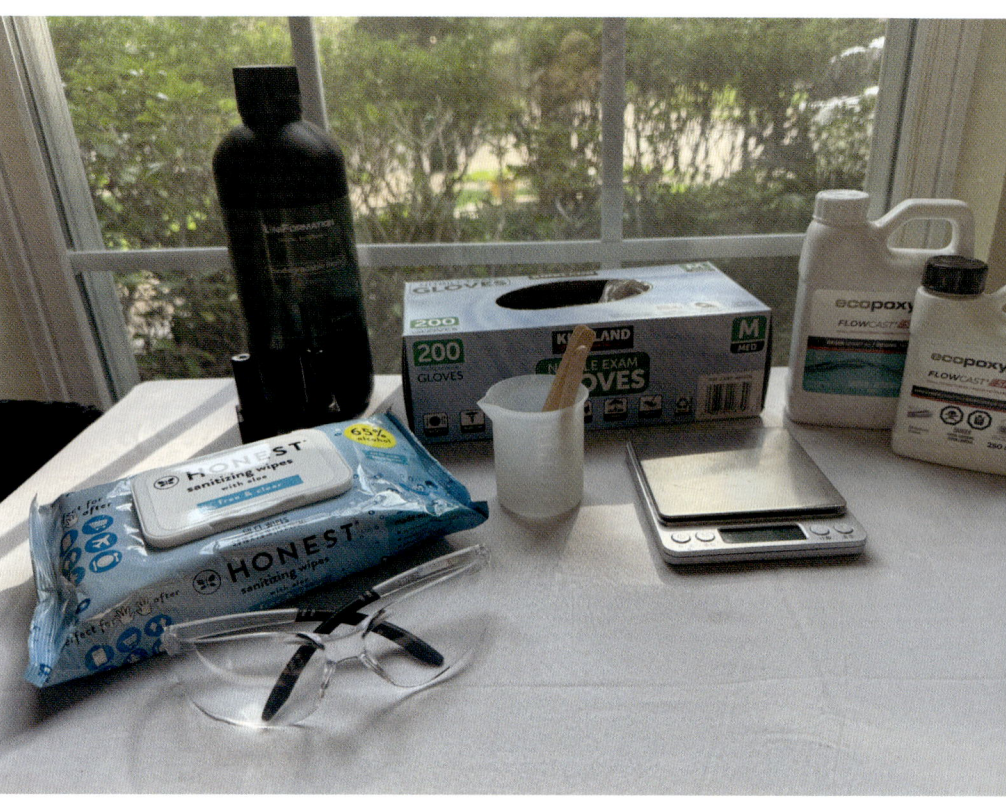

Handling resin

- Always read and follow the Materials Safety Data Sheet (MSDS) included with your specific resin product.
- Measure ingredients precisely to maintain the correct resin-to-hardener ratio.
- Organize tools like mixing sticks, cups, and gloves within reach to streamline your process.
- Resin drips and splashes will be very difficult to remove, so it's best to avoid the problem completely. If you do manage to get resin on the surface, clean it up immediately. Use wet wipes on your skin, followed by washing with soap and water. Use an alcohol wipe on your worksurface but avoid using them or any solvents on your skin.
- Do not eat, drink, or smoke while working with resin to prevent accidental ingestion.

- Store resin in sealed containers away from children and pets.
- Store resin components at recommended temperatures to prevent container pressurization.
- Dispose of resin properly. Follow manufacturer guidelines for disposing of unused resin and avoid pouring it down drains or in your regular garbage can.

Storage and disposal

- If using a two-component epoxy resin kit, keep both bottles tightly sealed and do not swap lids between Part A (silicone base) and Part B (curing agent).

Before you pour: tools and materials

The tools and materials you will need for the projects in this book are listed here.

Resin-specific tools

These tools are essential for preparing and working with both epoxy and UV resin. From precise measuring to safe handling and curing, they ensure consistent results and user safety. Items like UV lamps, mixing sticks, and coloring agents help customize each creation.

- 1.7 floz (50ml) squeeze bottle for larger amounts of resin
- Nail polish bottle with brush for applying small amounts and thin coatings
- Silicone base and curing agent
- UV Resin
- Wooden mixing sticks and plastic mixing cups
- Safety glasses
- Mask
- Digital scale
- Nitrile gloves

A

- Long-neck lighter
- UV lamp (A)
- Mica powder, alcohol ink, or coloring pigments (B)
- Nail polish topcoat (C)
- Nail file or sandpaper (D, E)
- Nail art stand (F)

B   C   D   E   F

Flower-drying tools

Preserving natural beauty starts with proper flower drying. Tools like silica gel, tweezers, and airtight containers help maintain delicate shapes and colors. A flower press offers flat and uniform drying, while curved scissors and sieves assist in precision and cleanup.

- Tweezers (**A**)
- Flower press
- Silica gel
- Sieve with handle
- Craft scissors
- Curved-tip scissors
- Foil-laminated plastic bag
- Airtight containers

Everyday tools and materials

These household staples play important roles in resin jewelry making. Silicone blocks create flat, stable, and non-stick bases; cotton swabs and alcohol sprays aid in cleaning; and tape and baby wipes help with preparation and finishing.

- Silicone or acrylic blocks (**B**)
- Plastic rod (**C**)
- Packing/craft tape (**D**)
- Cotton swab
- Paper towels
- Silicone mold (**E**)
- Powder brush (**F**)
- Baby wipes
- Rubbing alcohol in spray bottle (**G**)
- Alcohol wipes

A

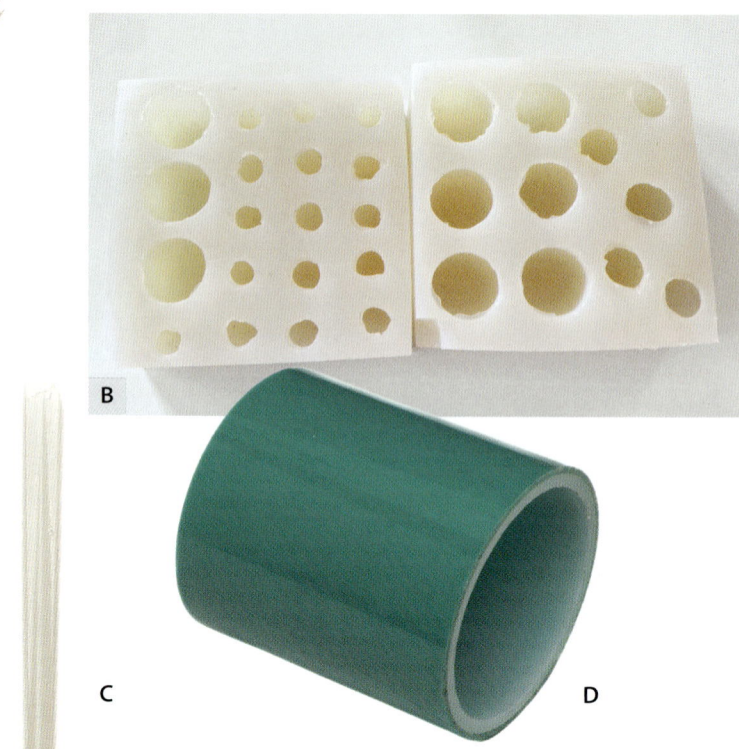

B

C

D

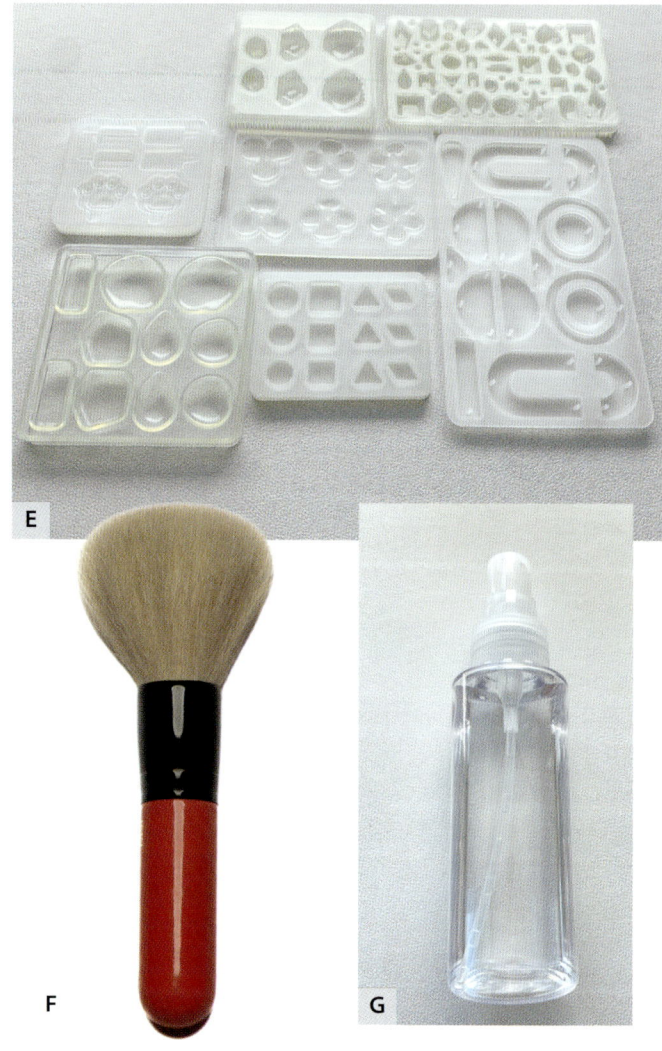

E

F

G

Jewelry essentials

These finishing components turn resin art into wearable pieces. Bezels, bails, pins, ear hooks, and chains form the structure, while pliers and drills are essential for easy assembly. Add personality with beads, crystals, and tassels to make unique jewelry pieces.

- Jewelry pliers
- Handheld drills
- Tailor's awl
- Bezels and frames
- Bails
- Ready-made necklaces, cut-to-order chains
- Eye pins, headpins, peg bails
- Jump rings
- Jump ring opener ring
- Earring backs
- Glue-on earring posts
- Ear hooks, earrings with attached rings
- Beads, crystals, pearls
- Wires
- Tassels

Basic resin techniques

Working with resin may seem intimidating at first, but with a few foundational techniques, you can create strong, clear, and beautiful pieces. This section introduces the essential methods every beginner should know – from preparing your workspace and mixing resin properly to pouring, curing, and finishing with confidence. Mastering these basics will give you the skills to explore more advanced designs later on, while avoiding common pitfalls along the way. Please refer to the Glossary on p.176 for definitions of some of the terms used throughout.

Accurate measuring and mixing of epoxy resin

- Pay close attention to the ratio specified in your resin's instructions. Confirm whether it is weight ratio or volume ratio.
- Use clear measuring cups or silicone jugs with marks for precise volume measurement.
- Calibrate scales and tare containers before weighing.
- Use disposable pipettes for small, precise pours.
- Always measure out the resin first and then add the hardener, not the other way around.
- Mix thoroughly but gently; avoid excessive air bubbles by stirring slowly and scraping the sides and bottom frequently.
- Once mixed, you have approximately 45 minutes of working time (depending on the resin you are using) before the product starts to cure, so start putting the resin into the setting without delay.

Avoiding and removing air bubbles

The best method for air bubble removal is to use a vacuum chamber to remove trapped air entirely. Alternatively, these are also effective ways to reduce or remove bubbles:

1. **Warm the resin:** Place the resin and hardener bottles in a warm water bath at 122–158°F (50–70°C) for 5–10 minutes before mixing. This reduces viscosity, allowing the bubbles to escape more easily.
2. **Mix slowly:** Stir the resin and hardener gently in a slow, deliberate motion. Avoid vigorous stirring, which traps air. Use a flat spatula and mix in figure-eight motions to ensure thorough blending without introducing bubbles.
3. **Pour slowly:** When pouring resin into molds, do so in thin, steady streams to minimize trapped air, especially for intricate designs.
4. **Use a heat source:** After pouring into the mold, use a heat gun or long-necked lighter to blow off bubbles on the surface for a few seconds. Do not use a torch on silicone molds as it will damage them.

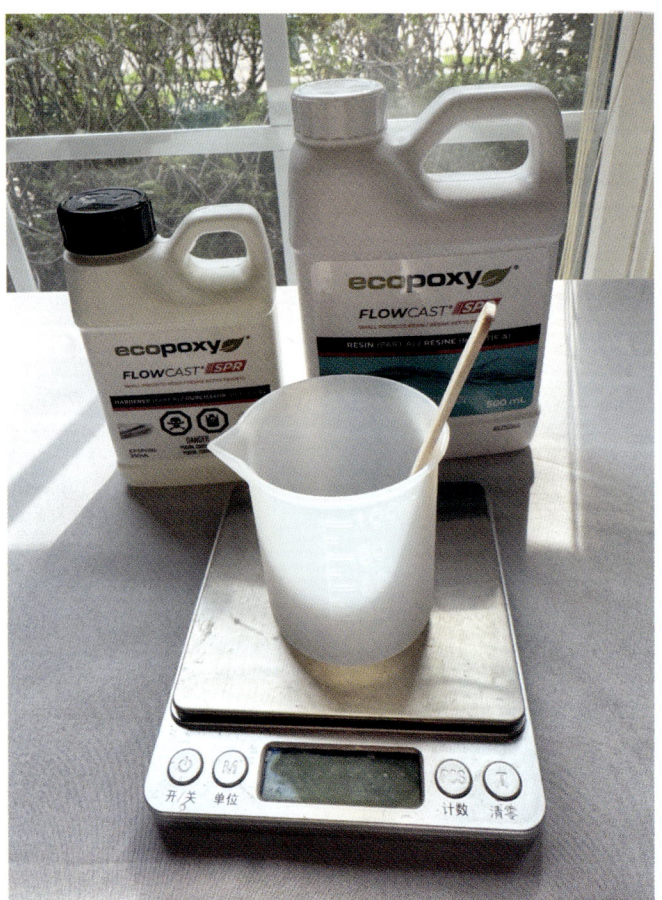

Above: **Vacuum chamber.**

Left : **Digital scales are essential for accurate measuring of the resins, component parts.**

Above: **Slightly overfilling the mold creates a dome that compensates for shrinkage during curing.**

Left: **Adding gold gravels for extra depth, color, and texture.**

Incorporating pigments and additives

- Combine dry pigments and alcohol ink with a little resin in a separate cup first, then combine the colored solution with the rest of the clear resin.
- Avoid moisture-containing materials; dry them before adding to the resin.

Filling a mold

When filling molds, ensure there is enough resin to form a slight dome to allow for shrinkage during the curing process. The dome will shrink to a flat surface once hardened. Filling just to level will result in a dip in the resin as it cures.

Curing

- The ideal curing temperature for epoxy resin is between 72°F (22°C) and 77°F (25°C).
- Cure times are usually 24 hours for hard cures and another 72 hours for full cures.
- Remove pieces from the mold after a 24-hour curing period. Should there be any minor surface imperfections, or you are dissatisfied with the

surface finish, it is recommended to apply a UV topcoat post-curing to achieve either a glossy or matte finish.
- Smooth rough edges with a nail file or sandpaper, then apply a thin layer of UV resin. Wet the piece or the sandpaper before starting. The dust produced can cause health issues if inhaled, so always wear a mask when sanding your work.

Silicone mold care

- Store molds flat in airtight plastic bags to prevent drying and deformation.
- Clean molds with mild soap and water; avoid harsh chemicals.
- Regularly inspect molds for wear and replace them when surfaces become dull or scratched.

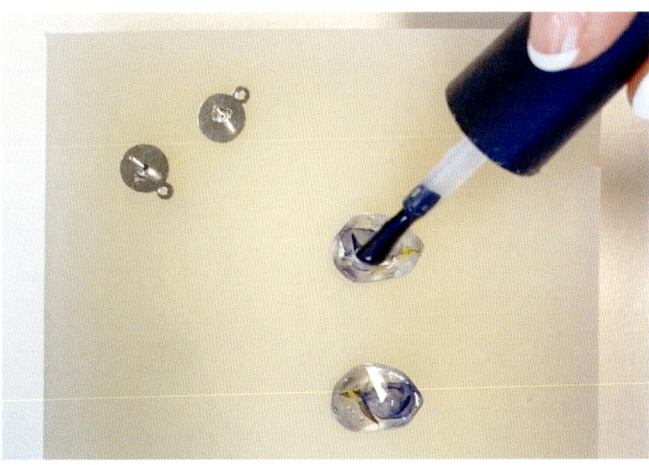

Above: **Applying a UV resin topcoat to a cured piece.**

Jewelry Tools and Findings

Every piece of resin jewelry you make is more than just resin and flowers – it's also shaped and finished with the help of the right tools and findings. Think of them as your creative companions: jewelry pliers that let you bend and shape metal with ease, and tiny but essential parts like jump rings, bezels, bails, and pins that connect, secure, and showcase your designs. These are the tools I keep close at hand on my worktable, and they've become trusted partners in my jewelry-making process.

At first glance, these tools and findings may look small and simple, but they play a big role in turning your cured resin pieces into wearable art. With just a few basic pliers and a small collection of findings, you can make endless creations. Over time, I've learned how even a single pair of pliers or the right size jump ring can make a big difference in how polished and professional a piece looks.

In this chapter, I'll walk you through the essentials you'll need in your toolkit, explain what each item is used for, and share tips for choosing and handling them. Whether you're new to jewelry making or looking to expand your skills, understanding these basics will make the project-making process run more smoothly.

Jewelry pliers

Jewelry pliers are essential tools for making and assembling jewelry. They provide precision, grip, and control when handling small components such as wire, jump rings, and beads.

Types of jewelry pliers

Jewelry pliers come in many different forms, most of them easily identifiable by a name that corresponds to their jaw shape.

- **Round-nose pliers:** Use these for looping wires and making jump rings (**A**).
- **Flat-nose pliers:** These have wide, flat jaws for holding, straightening, and flattening wire. They are often used for firm grips when opening or closing jump rings (**B**).
- **Chain-nose pliers:** These look similar to flat-nose pliers – round on the outside of the jaw but flat on the inside, tapering up to a point. The flat jaws allow for gripping, bending, and opening jump rings. They are useful for working in tight spaces and assembling small components.
- **Bent-nose pliers:** These are similar to chain-nose pliers but with angled jaws for better access to tight spaces. They are helpful for holding and manipulating small pieces without blocking your view.
- **Cutting pliers (flush cutters or side cutters):** These are designed for cutting wire, headpins, and excess metal. Flush cutters create a clean, flat cut, while side cutters make angled cuts (**C**).

Choosing the right pliers

Jewelry-making tools are easily purchased from your local craft shop, Amazon, and Etsy. To choose the right pliers for you, consider the following:

- **Material:** Look for stainless steel for durability.
- **Size:** Choose a smaller size if you have small hands.
- **Comfort:** Soft, ergonomic grips help reduce hand strain.
- **Cost:** If budget allows, select high-quality pliers from well-known brands.

Jewelry findings

This book uses commercially available jewelry findings from Etsy and the Japanese brand, Kiwa Seisakujo. The two most common materials used in these projects are:

1. **Sterling and gold-plated silver:** High-quality and tarnish-free – perfect for lightweight jewelry.
2. **Stainless steel and gold-plated stainless steel:** Strong, tarnish-resistant, hypoallergenic, and waterproof – great for durable jewelry.

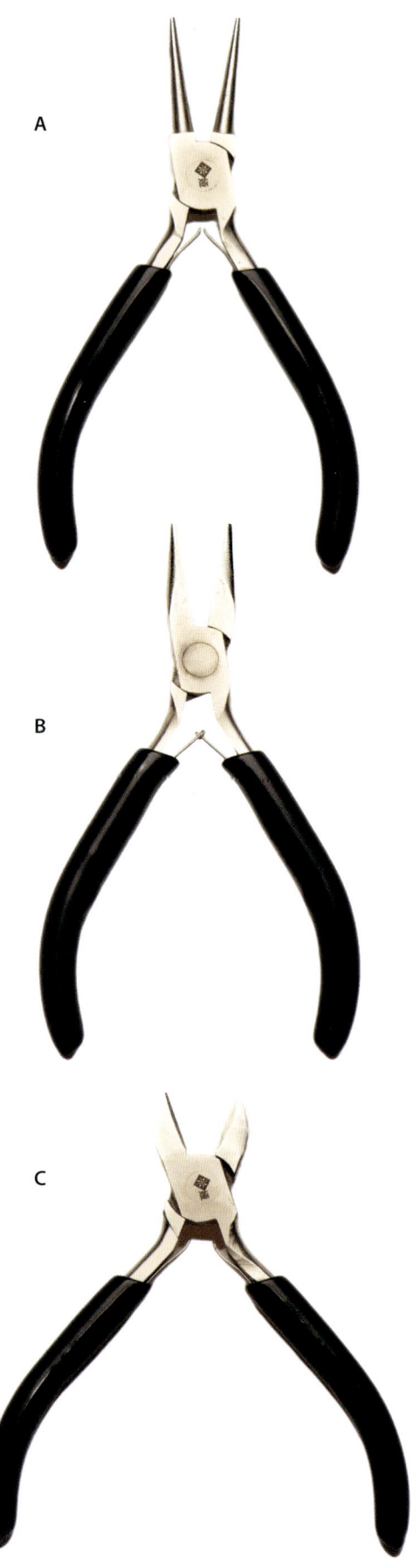

A

B

C

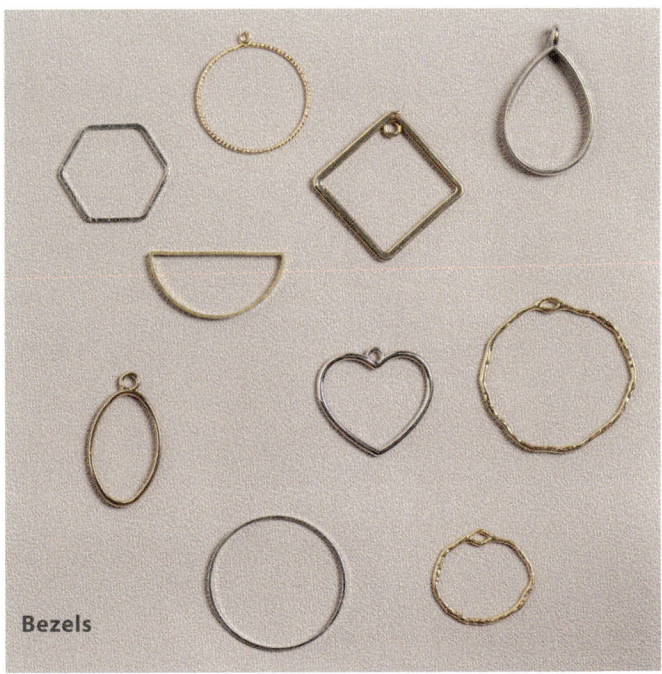

Bezels

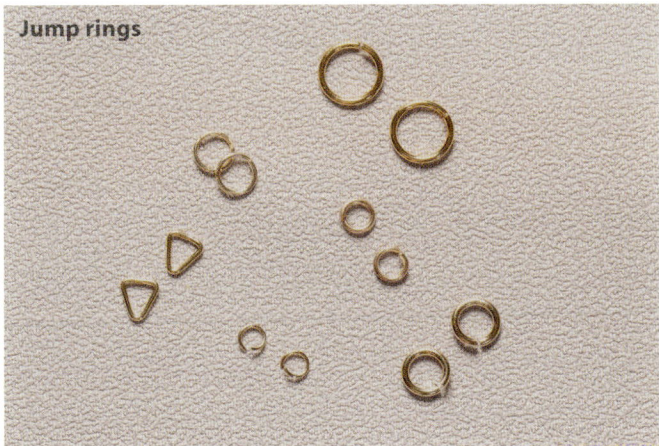

Jump rings

Jump rings by shape

- **Round jump rings:** The most common and versatile jump rings, used in almost all jewelry designs (**A, B**).
- **Oval jump rings:** More secure than round jump rings, as the opening sits on the side, reducing the chance of components slipping out.
- **Triangle jump rings:** Provide a unique geometric look and more surface contact for secure connections (**C**).

Jump rings by closure type

- **Open jump rings:** The most-used jump ring type. They have a small gap that can be opened and closed with pliers, making them easy to use but less secure (**D**).
- **Closed jump rings:** These are soldered shut for extra strength; commonly used in high-stress areas of jewelry (**E**).

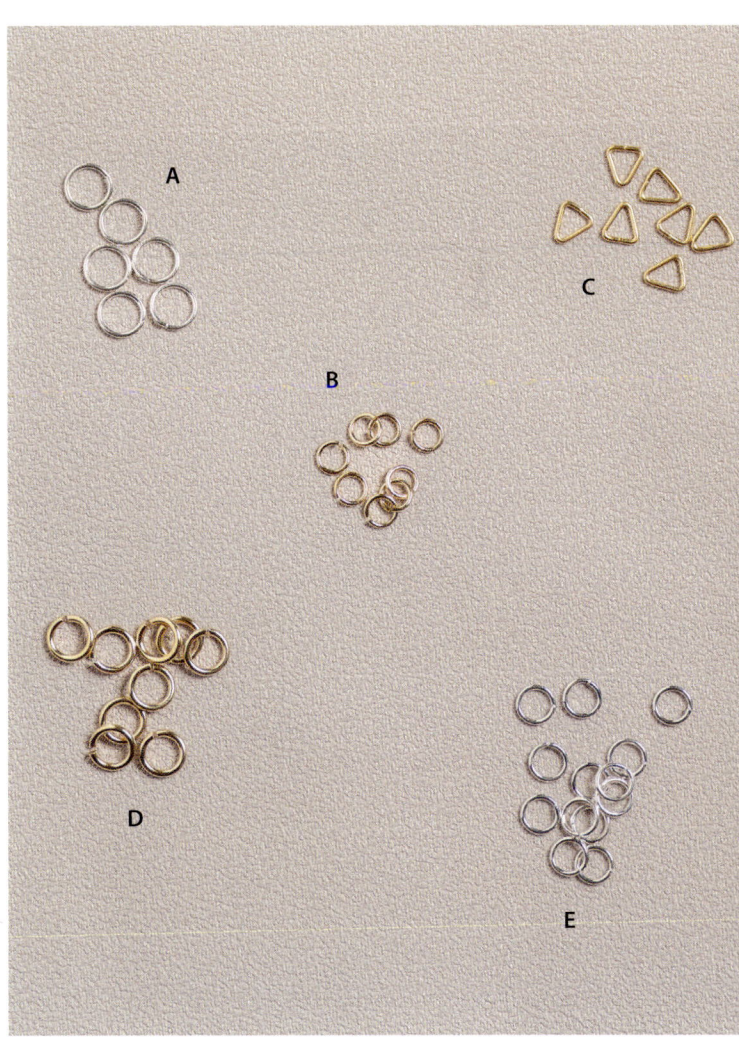

Open bezels

An open bezel is a frame without a backing, allowing the resin or material inside to be visible from both sides. It's perfect for transparent resin jewelry because it allows light through, creates a floating effect, and is lightweight.

Jump rings

Jump rings are essentially wire circles. They are one of the simplest ways to connect jewelry components together. To open and close a jump ring, use two flat-nose pliers to move its ends apart without distorting its shape. Open it just enough to insert the objects being joined to maintain its shape and strength.

Jump ring size

Jump rings are measured by:

- **Inner diameter:** The space inside the ring. Between 4mm and 6mm is the most-used size in this book.
- **Wire gauge (thickness):** Wire is measured in either millimeters (UK measurement guide) or in gauge (US measurement guide), starting at 32 gauge (0.2mm) and ranging to 6 gauge (4mm). The most common gauges used in this book are 20–22 gauge (0.6-0.8mm), which are best for lightweight charms and delicate jewelry.

Jump ring opener

A jump ring opener is a small, ring-shaped tool worn on your finger – usually the index finger. It is used to easily open and close jump rings when making jewelry.

Opening jump rings by hand with pliers can be fiddly or uneven. The jump ring opener simplifies this process. To use the jump ring opener:

1. Slide the jump ring into one of the slits on the opener.
2. Use pliers to twist the jump ring against the slit – one hand holds the pliers; the other rotates the ring.
3. This twists the jump ring open (but does not pull it apart), keeping it properly aligned and round.

Above: **Inserting a jump ring into the drilled hole of purple primrose earrings (see p.67).**

4. After attaching your components, reverse the twist to close it.

Bails

Bails allow pendants to be attached to chains or cords. Here are a few types of bails I frequently use in this book:

Glue-on bails

A flat-backed bail that attaches directly to a pendant using strong adhesive, such as E6000 or UV resin. It's one of the easiest bails to use (**A**).

- **Pros:** Quick and easy to use, available in many styles.
- **Cons:** Requires strong adhesive and may not work well for heavy pendants.

Snap-on or pinch bails

A decorative bail with two small prongs that pinch into a drilled hole in a pendant. These bails provide a professional look while securely holding the pendant in place (**B**).

- **Pros:** Secure, elegant, no glue needed.
- **Cons:** Need to drill a through hole in the resin pendants.

Bails

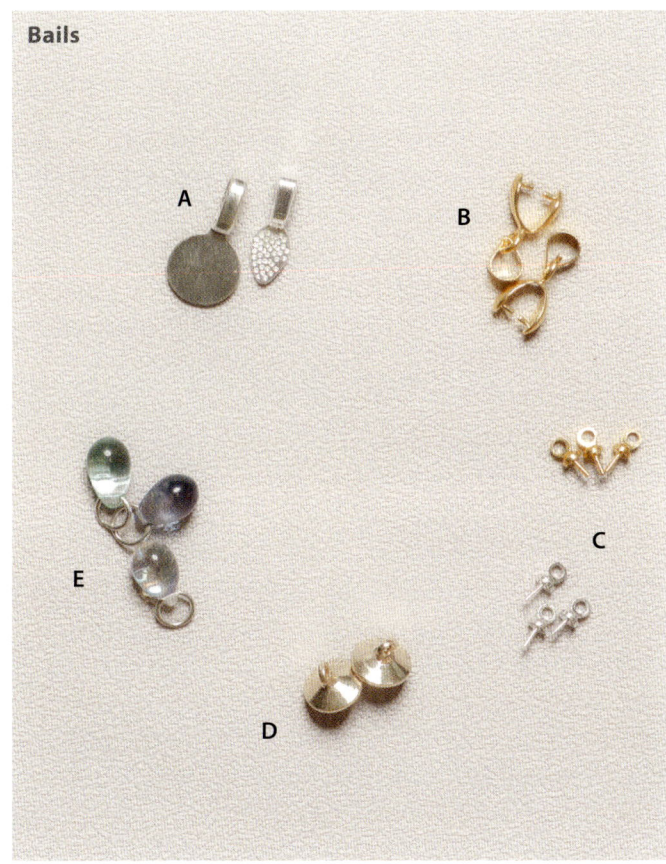

Also consider the overall aesthetic. Some bails are more decorative, while others are minimal and hidden. Choose one that complements your jewelry design.

Eye pins and Headpins

Both eye pins and headpins (also called T-pins) are essential in jewelry making, especially when working with beads, pearls, and charms. Eye pins are great for linking elements together, while T-pins are perfect for creating dangling beads and charms.

Eye pins

An eye pin is a straight metal wire with a small loop (or "eye") at one end (H, I). This loop makes it easy to attach the pin to chains, jump rings, or other jewelry components.

- **Bead links:** String a bead or charm onto the pin, then create a second loop at the other end with round-nose pliers. This turns the pin into a connector for linking multiple components (K).
- **Dangles and charms:** Attach a decorative bead or resin piece to the eye pin, then connect the loop to an earring hook, bracelet, or necklace (L).
- **Chain extensions:** Eye pins can be linked together to create a beaded chain effect, making them perfect for delicate and decorative designs (J).

Screw-in bails (peg bails)

A bail with a small peg or screw that inserts into a drilled hole in the pendant, often secured with glue for extra hold. 3 x 6.9mm and 4 x 7.2mm are the sizes I use the most (C, D).

- **Pros:** Secure, durable, great for thicker pendants.
- **Cons:** Requires drilling

Jump ring bails

A simple bail created by attaching a jump ring through a pendant's hole. This is one of the most basic ways to hang a pendant, but it works well for lightweight pieces (E).

- **Pros:** Easy to attach, great for small pieces.
- **Cons:** need to drill through holes, less decorative, not ideal for heavy pendants.

When selecting a bail for your handmade jewelry, consider pendant weight and size. A sturdy bail is necessary for heavier pendants, while smaller, more delicate bails work for lightweight pieces. A bigger pendant is a better visual match with a bigger bail. A heavier pendant works better with pinch or snap-on bails.

Eye pins

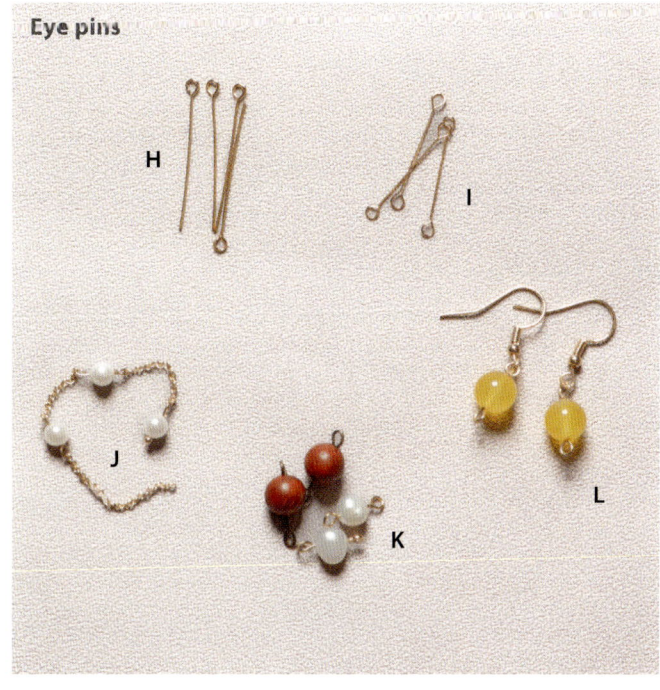

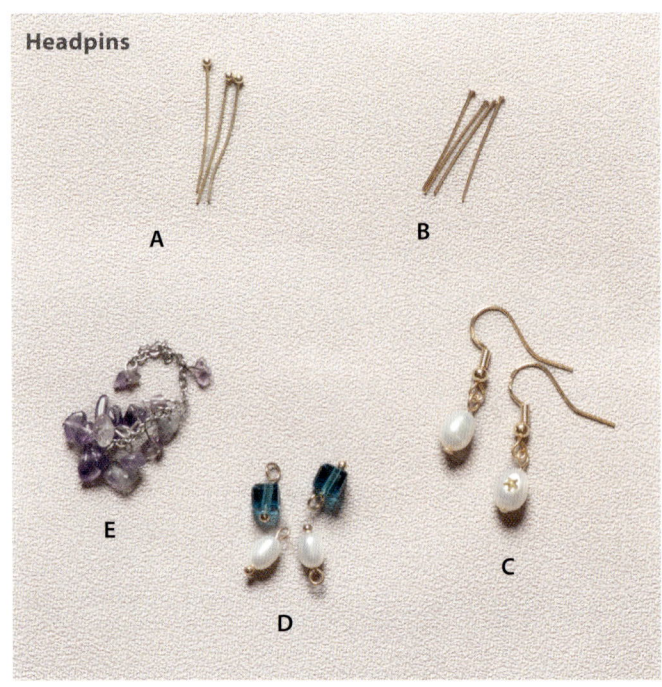

Headpins

A   B

E

D   C

Earring components

Handmade jewelry designers have a variety of earring backs to choose from, each offering different levels of security and style. Here's a breakdown of the most used types and how to select the best one for your designs.

Ear wires/French hooks

French hooks, also known as shepherd's hooks, are curved wires that loop through the earlobe and dangle freely. They are among the most commonly used earring hooks in handmade jewelry because of their ease of wear and classic look.

Glue-on ear posts

Glue-on ear posts are flat-backed metal posts that attach directly to the back of an earring design using UV resin or jewelry adhesive. They come in various diameters (e.g., 4mm, 6mm, 8mm, 10mm), shapes, and metal finishes. Glue-on ear posts are one of the simplest and most popular findings used to create stud earrings in handmade jewelry.

Earring backs

These secure earrings in place. Types include butterfly, screw, and push backs.

Headpins (T-pins)

A headpin is a straight metal wire with a flat end, ball end, or decorative head that prevents beads from slipping off (**A, B**).

A headpin can be used to create the following designs and structures:

- **Beaded drops:** Secure a bead onto the pin and form a loop at the top (**D**).
- **Dangling beads and charms:** String beads onto the headpin, then bend the opposite end into a loop with pliers to attach it to earrings, pendants, or bracelet chains (**C**).
- **Cluster designs:** Create clusters of beads by attaching multiple beaded headpins onto a jump ring or earring hook for a decorative, dangling effect (**E**).

Table 3: Comparison between an eye pin and headpin

	Eye pin	Headpin (T-pin)
End type	Loop (eye)	Flat or decorative end
Best for	Connecting elements, chain links	Creating dangles, drop beads
Loop needed?	Already has one	Must create one for attachment
Common use	Bead links, charm connections	Earrings, dangling pendants, clustered beads

Ear wires/French hooks

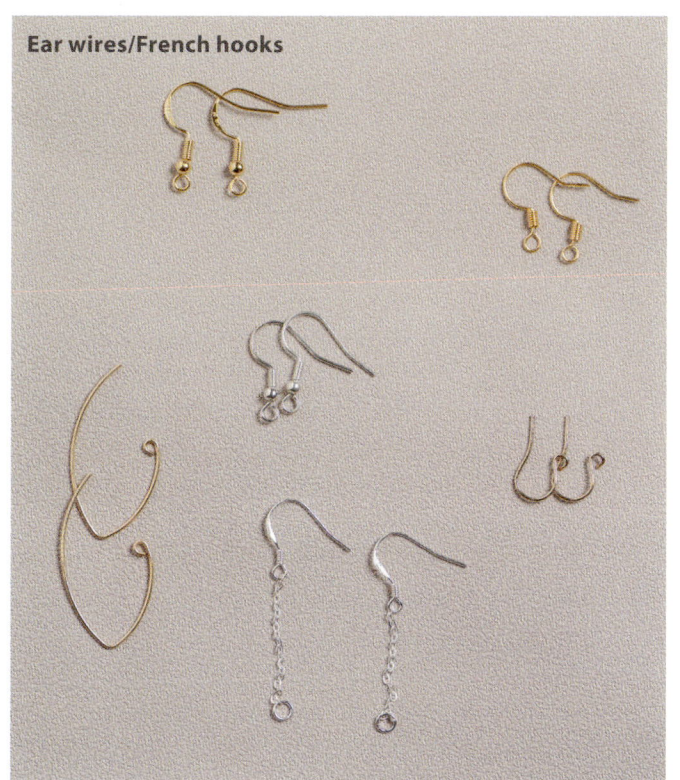

Glue-on ear posts

Earring backs

Table 4: Comparison between various earring backs

Type	Best for	Security	Comfort
Butterfly clutch	Studs, lightweight dangles	Medium	Medium
Silicone back	Lightweight, sensitive ears	Low–medium	High
Bullet clutch	Heavy earrings	Medium–high	High
Fish hook and stopper	Open hook earrings	Medium	High

Chains

It's best to choose a fine chain for simple and light-weight pieces and a heavy chain for designs that require more strength, such as a design featuring a large pendant. A heavy design usually comes with a sturdy lobster clasp; a light and delicate chain typically comes with a bolt ring clasp.

The length of a necklace chain is a personal preference, with 16in (41cm) and 18in (46cm) being the most common. I frequently use 16–18in (41–46cm) adjustable chains in my designs. Larger pendants work well with both short and long chains, while delicate designs are better suited to shorter chains.

If you are using sterling silver components (bezels, jump rings, or bails, for example), I recommend using the same material for your chain.

One of the nice things about chains is that styles vary so widely that you can really set the tone of a design through your chain choice.

Ready-made chains

Ready-made chains are available commercially. They have a clasp attached already and are available in various gauges and lengths (A).

I use ready-made chains for my necklace designs. I also purchase cut-to-order loose chains to be used in my dangling earrings, which I cut to my desired length (B, C). Chains are used in making bracelets too, where I need to add my own clasps and findings.

Cable chains

Cable chains are a timeless, simple style that consists of identical round or oval links connected in a continuous sequence.

Cable chains are the classic image most people have in their mind when they think of chains. If you're not sure which chain to go for, these are great basic chains to start with.

Box chains

Box chains are characterized by square-shaped links connected to form a continuous chain. This structure provides a modern look and a sturdy foundation. The clean lines of the box chain make it an excellent choice for minimalist designs.

Charm chains

Charm chains have gems or pearls along the chain. They are good for decorative pieces (D).

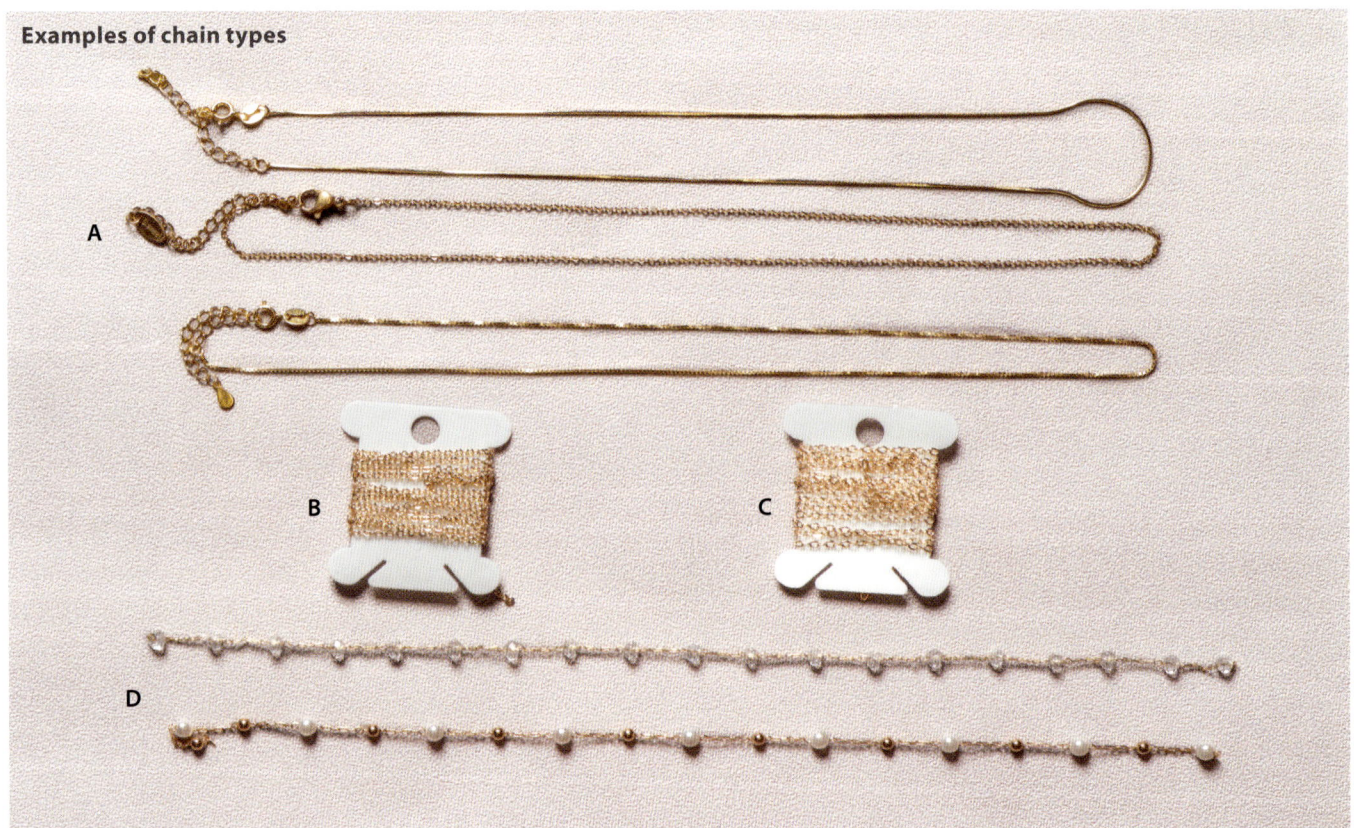

Examples of chain types

A

B

C

D

Beads, pearls, and tassels

Beads, pearls, and tassels not only add visual interest and texture, but they also carry rich cultural and artisanal significance. Incorporating these components into your handmade jewelry opens up endless creative possibilities. You can combine modern resin techniques with natural and artisanal materials to create storytelling pieces.

Beads

Incorporating beads into resin jewelry can be an excellent way to add structure and vibrant pops of color. For example, a blue seed bead might be connected to a blue flower design to enhance the color theme. A larger gemstone bead can serve as a focal point that draws the eye.

Beads can be embedded in resin together with the flowers to create intricate, almost mosaic-like

Glass and seed beads

Gemstone and crystal beads

Wood, metal, and ceramic beads

patterns. However, in some cases, cured resin often obscures the facets of loose crystal gems, causing them to disappear inside the piece.

Glass and seed beads

These small, uniform beads are perfect for detailed work and intricate patterns. They can be found in nearly every color and finish, allowing you to create delicate designs or bold contrasts.

Gemstone and crystal beads

There are so many choices these days, from semi-precious stones to high-quality crystals. These beads bring a touch of elegance and sparkle to your pieces.

Wood, metal, and ceramic beads

Wood beads can be used for a more organic and natural feel. Metal alloys and ceramics can be used to create a contrast with flowers. These materials can introduce texture and depth to designs that incorporate the transparency of resin and the softness of natural flowers.

Pearls

Cultured freshwater pearls are the most common pearls available today, appreciated for their consistent luster and smooth finish. When used in resin jewelry, pearls can add an unexpected pop of sophistication. They work well as embedded accents within resin or as pendants that complement the organic charm of preserved flowers, creating a harmonious balance between nature and refined craftsmanship.

Tassels

The dangling, free-flowing nature of tassels brings a dynamic and playful motion to jewelry, catching the light and drawing the eye with every subtle movement. Traditionally made from threads like silk, cotton, or synthetic fibers, tassels can be both a design element and a symbol of artistic freedom.

Pearls

Tassels

Other embellishments

Other natural or eco-friendly embellishments used in this book include:

Crushed glass gravels

Gold and silver-coated varieties are used most frequently, though multicolored options are also available.

Mica-based glitters

Primarily gold and silver tones are featured, with additional colors available.

Metal foil shavings

18k gold and silver-coated versions are most common, while rose gold and 14k gold options are also used.

Crushed glass gravels

Mica-based glitters

Metal foil shavings

Preparing Botanical Components

Before flowers can be set in resin, they need to be preserved in a way that maintains their beauty, structure, and color. Fresh blooms, while vibrant, will quickly fade and lose their form if not prepared correctly. That's why learning different drying and preservation techniques is an essential first step for resin artists.

In this chapter, we'll explore several methods of preparing flowers, each with its own advantages. Flower pressing flattens blooms into paper-thin forms, perfect for creating delicate botanical silhouettes. Air-drying is the simplest method, giving flowers a soft, rustic look. Drying with silica gel preserves both shape and vibrancy, making it ideal for colorful, lifelike pieces. Freeze-drying captures the flower's form and color with remarkable precision, creating a near-perfect replica of the fresh bloom. Finally, "forever flowers" – professionally preserved blooms that are treated to last – offer a convenient option when you want consistent quality without the work of drying them yourself. By understanding these approaches, you'll be able to select the best method for your creative jewelry projects.

Pressing flowers

Several methods for pressing flowers have developed over time. I do not recommend book pressing as it is inefficient and sometimes causes the flowers to become moldy. I also discourage microwave pressing as it is difficult to control the process to reach complete dryness without scorching the flowers.

The wooden flower press

I use a commercial wooden flower press with liner paper and a drying plate made with absorbent materials (such flower presses can be easily purchased on Amazon). A more specialized press will come with pre-drilled holes and bolts and wing nuts for applying even pressure.

A wooden flower press typically consists of the following components:

- **Two flat pressing plates:** Usually made of wood, these provide the structure and apply pressure to the flowers.
- **Drying plates:** These layers absorb moisture from the flowers. The absorbent plates will become soft after use. They will need to be dried using a microwave for the next use.
- **Foam sheet:** This is placed between the absorbent sheets to allow airflow and even pressure distribution.

Assembled flower press.

- **Liner paper:** This keeps flowers separated from the drying plate to avoid them staining it.
- **Bolts and wingnuts (or straps/clamps):** These tighten the press, applying consistent pressure to flatten and dry the flowers evenly.

Components: two flat pressing plates, drying plates, foam sheets, liner paper, bolts and wingnuts. Also shown: tweezers and scissors.

How to press flowers

Here is the step-by-step process of pressing flowers:

1. Choose flowers that are fresh and dry (avoid flowers with dew or moisture, or that are wilting), and without blemishes (**A**). Flat flowers such as pansies press easily, while thicker flowers like roses may need to be split in half or some petals removed.

2. Place a layer of drying plate on the wood plate. Apply a liner paper (**B**).

3. Use tweezers to lay the flowers flat and space them apart on the paper (**C**). Apply another liner paper.

4. Apply a foam sheet (**D**).

A

B

C

D

5. Place another layer of drying plate (**E**).

6. Put the stack in a plastic bag with a zip seal (**F**).

7. Place a heavy weight on top of the plate (**G**). Alternatively, if you use a strap flower press, tighten the straps or use a screw and bolt to tighten the whole stack. Store the press in a dry, cool place for 3–5 days, depending on flower thickness. If you are pressing thick flowers, replace the drying plate every few days to speed up drying. Failing to replace damp paper can lead to mold growth.

8. Once fully dried, carefully remove the flowers with tweezers (**H**).

Above: **Air-dried oak leaves, purple statice and dyed baby's breath flowers.**

9. Place the flowers in a resealable bag (I). Put the resealable bags in airtight containers with desiccant, such as silica gel.

10. Regenerate the drying plates by placing them in the microwave for 3–5 minutes until dry. They should feel dry and stiff when fully dried. Apply microwave power in 1-minute intervals and check the board after each minute.

Tips on pressing flowers

- Avoid regular paper towels or textured paper that may stick to or imprint on the flowers.
- Avoid overcrowding; leave space between the flowers for even drying.
- Apply correct pressure: too much pressure can crush delicate petals, while too little can result in uneven drying.
- Rushing the process can lead to incomplete drying and potential mold growth. If pressing thick flowers, change the absorbent paper after two days.
- Use nylon tweezers to handle delicate pressed flowers to avoid tearing them.

Air-drying flowers

Air-drying is one of the simplest and most natural methods of preserving flowers. This technique involves hanging flowers upside down in a dry, well-ventilated space, slowly removing moisture while maintaining their structure.

How to air-dry flowers

Air-drying is the simplest, most eco-friendly method of drying flowers. All my lavender, baby's breath (natural and dyed), and yellow and purple statice are dried in this way. Choose fresh flowers with minimal moisture – mini roses, lavender, baby's breath, and statice dry well.

To air-dry flowers, first prepare them by removing excess leaves and then bundle small groups with twine or rubber bands. Suspend the flowers upside down in a dark, dry, well-ventilated space to prevent mold and fading, and let them dry for one to three weeks (drying times vary depending on humidity and flower type).

41

Forever flowers

Forever flowers are real flowers that undergo a special preservation process in which the moisture in the flowers is replaced by a glycerin-based solution, allowing them to maintain their fresh appearance and soft texture for an extended period. Unlike dried or artificial flowers, forever flowers retain their natural look and feel. Some flowers or leaves are dyed to achieve vibrant or unique colors.

Due to the highly specialized nature of the process used to make flowers last forever, they usually cannot be made at home. They can be easily purchased on Etsy and Amazon. Hydrangeas are the most common forever flowers used in resin flower jewelry.

Left: **Air-drying baby's breath flowers removes moisture while maintaining their delicate structure and charm.**

Below: **These hydrangea forever flowers are a popular choice for both resin jewelry and long-lasting floral decor.**

Above : **Freeze-dried flowers are lifelike and three-dimensional.**

Freeze-dried flowers

Freeze-drying (lyophilization) is also a great way to preserve botanical elements like flowers, leaves, and fruit slices. It is a dehydration process where flowers are frozen at extremely low temperatures (-40°F/-40°C or below). They are placed in a vacuum chamber, where moisture is removed by sublimation (solid to gas transition), then slowly dried to preserve their natural color, shape, and texture.

Freeze-dried flowers retain a three-dimensional appearance and experience less shrinkage or discoloration. However, they are very fragile and can crumble if not handled carefully. Creating high-quality freeze-dried flowers independently is not feasible, but freeze-dried fruit slices and petals can be readily purchased online.

Above : **A plastic tub used for storing dried flowers.**

Storing dried flowers

To help preserve the beauty and integrity of dried flowers for your projects and keepsakes, keep them away from sunlight and heat. To prevent mold on pressed flowers, use airtight containers with silica gel or other desiccants to absorb moisture.

Freeze-dried flowers and fruit slices absorb moisture more than pressed flowers. Make sure to store them in a sealed, aluminum foil-laminated bag placed in an airtight container.

Drying flowers with silica gel

Using silica gel is a popular and effective method for drying and preserving flowers, offering several advantages over traditional air-drying techniques. This process allows flowers to retain their shape, color, and texture for extended periods. Silica gel is a desiccant that rapidly absorbs moisture from flowers, preventing wilting and fading. The tiny pores in silica gel can absorb up to 40 percent of moisture from the surrounding environment, making it ideal for flower preservation.

Right: **Texas wildflowers in a tub filled with silica gel.**

Below: **Tools for drying flowers with silica gel:** aluminum-foil-lined plastic bag, tweezers, scissors, and sieve.

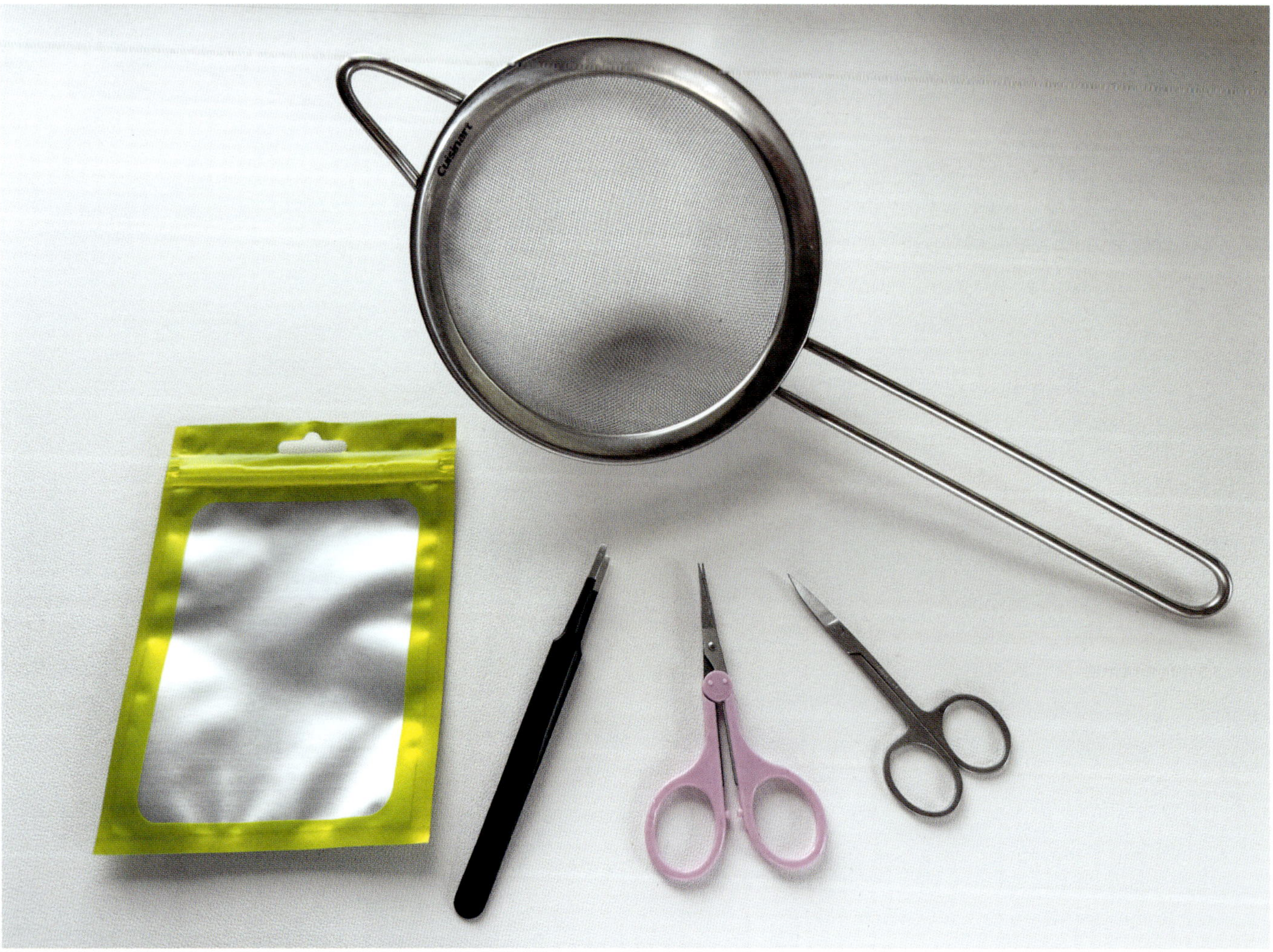

How to dry flowers using silica gel

1. Select fresh flowers at their peak bloom, ensuring they are free from moisture before drying. Trim the stems.

2. Pour a 1–2in (2.5–5cm) layer of silica gel into an airtight container. Use fine silica gel sand rather than beads or crystals for better results (A).

3. Place the flowers face down on the silica gel (B, C).

4. Gently pour silica gel over and between the petals (D).

5. Seal the container and store at room temperature (E). Check after 2–6 days, depending on the flower type.

6. Carefully remove the flowers with a slotted spoon and brush off any excess gel (F). Handle dried flowers with care, as they can be fragile. Recharge silica gel by heating it in the oven when the color indicator shows moisture absorption (for example, blue crystals turning pink).

Flower petals and stems carefully arranged for pressing, spaced evenly on liner paper and handled gently to preserve their shape and color. Proper pressing transforms fresh blooms into delicate, paper-thin botanical forms which are perfect for resin art.

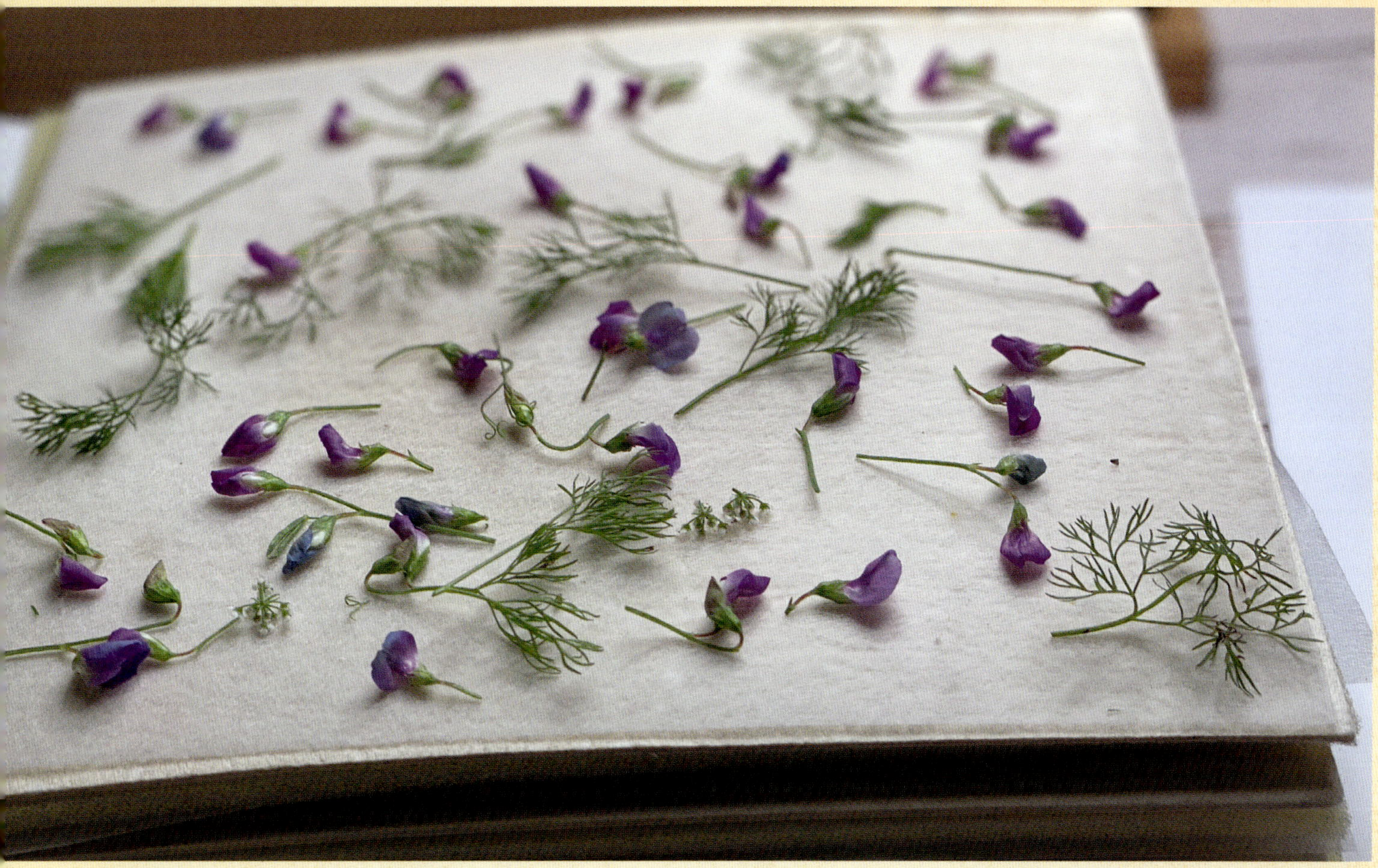

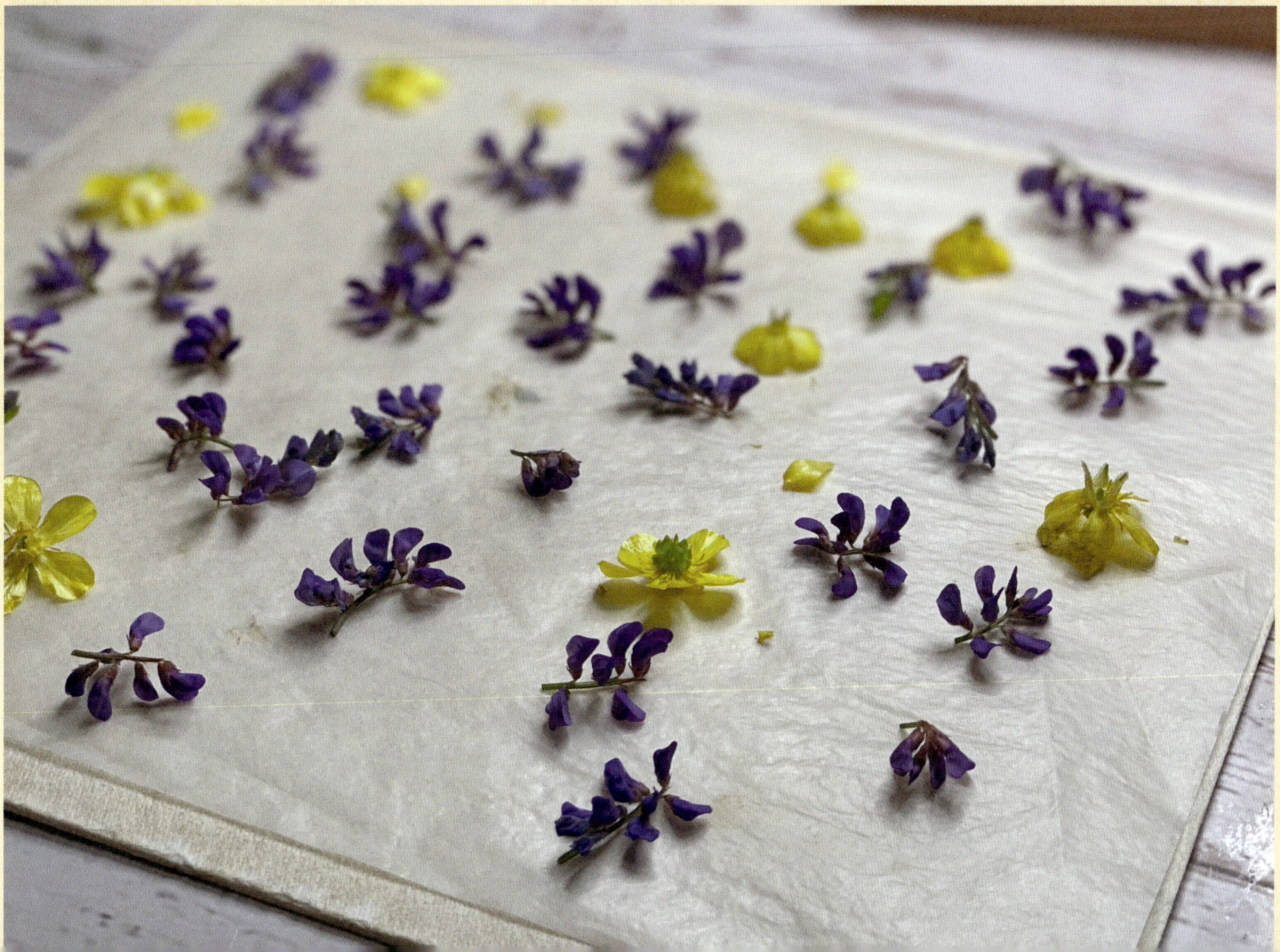

Flower Encapsulation

Encapsulation is a beautifully minimal yet technically intricate method of making resin flower jewelry. The projects in this chapter use only dried flowers and resin, with no molds, bezels, or frames. Each piece is built up by carefully hand-applying resin to completely cover the flower, preserving its natural beauty and shape in crystal-clear layers.

Jewelry made using the encapsulation method is the most lightweight, making it especially suitable for earrings and delicate pendants. Although the process may seem simple, a practiced hand is required to achieve the ideal thickness: thin enough to maintain the flower's delicate structure, yet thick enough to provide strength and stability.

The technique used in this chapter is arguably the simplest of all methods in this book, relying on only resin, flowers, and hand tools. However, some of the projects involving multilayer stacking of resin and flower elements can be difficult. They require precise alignment, curing times, and visual balance.

Flower encapsulation best practice

Because the flowers remain fragile until fully coated, always handle them with tweezers to prevent tearing or crumbling. The first layer of resin should be applied as thinly as possible; thicker coats generate more heat during curing, which can cause the petals to curl or distort.

You can apply resin using various tools: small acrylic paintbrushes, silicone brushes, toothpicks, or plastic sticks. Choose the tool that feels most natural to you. However, if you use a traditional paintbrush, be sure to clean it immediately after the project – before the resin cures – using acetone or alcohol. This will preserve the brush for future use.

Projects in this chapter typically require a silicone block to keep the flower flat while curing. Most pieces also need a hand drill to create connection points, and a soft bristle brush to clean off dust from drilling. Without molds to shape the design, precision and patience are essential throughout.

Unless stated otherwise, the recommended cure time under a UV lamp is two minutes per layer, as plant-based UV resin typically requires slightly longer to cure fully.

For all the encapsulation projects in this chapter, include a final inspection step before attaching the jewelry findings. Inspect each piece for any remaining bubbles, uneven surfaces, or imperfec-tions. If needed, apply a final thin layer of UV resin to smooth out any spots and cure it under the UV lamp. Check the edges carefully – if any areas feel sharp or rough, gently file them down and apply a thin layer of resin to reseal those edges. Cure again to ensure a clean, polished finish before proceeding to attach findings like jump rings or ear hooks.

For projects using glue on a flat pad earring post, always begin by slightly roughening the resin surface where the glue will go. This improves the adhesive bond. Then, clean the pad thoroughly with rubbing alcohol or mild soap to remove any oils, dust, or residue before attaching the decorative piece.

Project 1:

Whole marigold earrings

These earrings feature the striking bright orange of marigold petals, making them a true statement piece full of warmth and energy. Marigolds are thicker flowers, so when pressing them, it helps to remove a few petals first and replace the absorbent plate with a fresh one after three days, then continuing to dry for another three. The result is a vibrant, flat bloom ready for resin work. Their striking color makes these earrings perfect for festive occasions, celebrations, or whenever you want to add a touch of bold elegance to your outfit.

You will need

- ✿ Pressed whole marigold flowers
- ✿ Silicone block
- ✿ UV resin
- ✿ Plastic rod, toothpick, or needle
- ✿ UV lamp
- ✿ Nail file or sandpaper
- ✿ Stiff foam block or any cushion for drilling
- ✿ Small handheld jewelry drill
- ✿ Powder brush
- ✿ Jewelry pliers (flat nose)
- ✿ Jewelry findings (two 0.7 x 6mm jump rings, two ear hooks all in gold-plated stainless steel)

1. Place a marigold flower on a silicone block. The silicone block helps keep the flower flat during curing and allows any spilled resin to be easily removed after it hardens.

2. Apply a thin layer of UV resin over the flower (**A**). Avoid applying too thick a layer, as excess heat during curing can cause the petals to curl.

3. Use a plastic rod, toothpick, or needle to spread the resin evenly and remove any bubbles (**B**).

4. Place the silicone block with the coated flower under a UV lamp and cure for 2 minutes (**C**).

5. Add another thin layer of UV resin to even out the surface (**D**). Cure again for 2 minutes.

6. Flip the flower over and coat the back with a thin layer of resin. Spread it evenly and cure for another 2 minutes.

7. Add another thin layer of UV resin to even out the surface and cure again for 2 minutes.

8. Inspect both sides of the flower for thin spots or uneven coverage. Apply more resin where needed (**E**). Cure again to ensure a smooth finish.

9. Repeat Steps 1–8 for the second marigold flower so you have a matching pair for the earrings.

10. Once both flowers are fully coated and cured, inspect for any remaining bubbles or rough edges. If needed, apply a final thin coat of resin and cure again.

11. Gently smooth any sharp areas using a nail file or sandpaper. Seal with a small amount of resin, then cure once more.

12. Place the marigold on the stiff foam block or cushion. Use a handheld jewelry drill to make a small hole near the top of each flower, about 3mm from the edge (**F**).

13. Use the powder brush to brush off any dust that has been generated from the drilling (**G**).

14. Use a pair of flat-nosed jewelry pliers to insert a jump ring through each hole and then to attach an ear hook to each jump ring (**H**).

Project 2:

Half marigold earrings

These earrings feature a playful twist on the classic marigold by using only half of the bloom, showing off the green stem for a fresh, lively vibe. While still bold and eye-catching, the smaller size makes them feel more energetic and versatile. When pressing the half marigold, remove as much of the flower center as possible and change the absorbent plate around day three to ensure even drying. This design works beautifully for casual outings or festive occasions, offering a statement piece that's both bright and fun.

You will need

- Two pressed half marigold flowers
- Silicone block
- UV resin
- Plastic rod, toothpick, or needle
- UV lamp
- Nail file or sandpaper
- Small handheld jewelry drill
- Stiff foam block or any cushion for drilling
- Powder brush
- Jewelry pliers (flat nose)
- Jewelry findings (two ear hooks, two 0.7 x 6mm jump rings all in gold-plated stainless steel)

1. Place the first flower on a silicone block. Pick a side to start with – either is fine.

2. Apply a thin layer of UV resin over the flower (A). Avoid thick coats, as excessive heat from curing can cause curling.

3. Spread the resin evenly with a plastic rod, toothpick, or needle to cover all parts of the flower (B).

4. Place the silicone block under a UV lamp (C). Cure the flower for 2 minutes.

5. Add a second thin layer of resin to even out the surface. Cure under the UV lamp for another 2 minutes.

6. Once the front side is complete, flip the flower over and repeat the resin coating and curing steps on the back.

7. Inspect the flower for any areas with thin or uneven resin. Apply a small amount of resin to those spots and cure again to achieve a smooth, even finish.

A

B

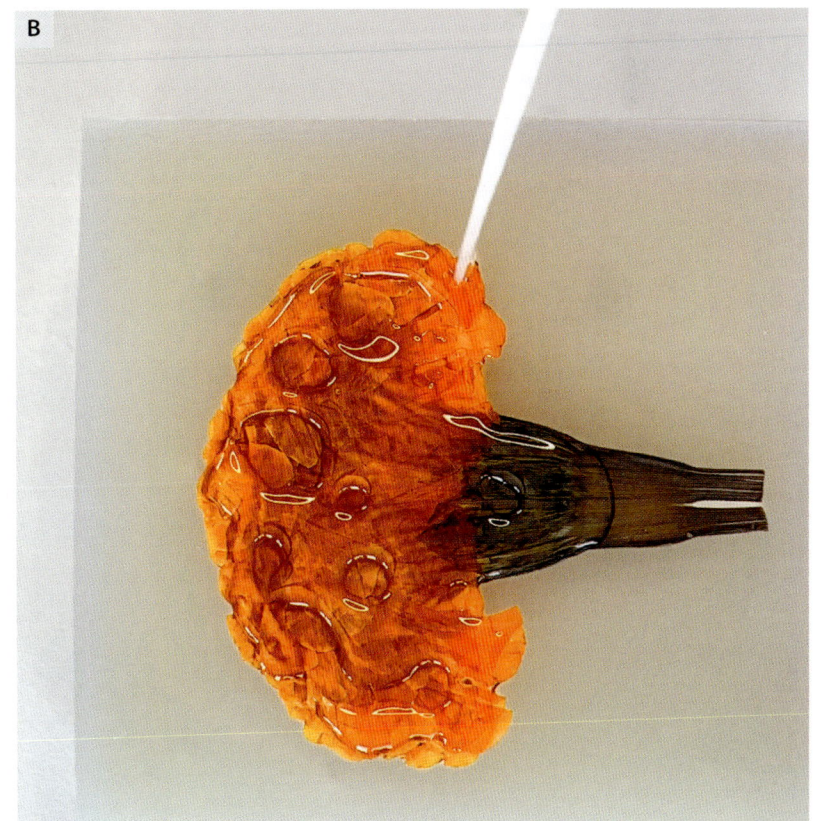

C

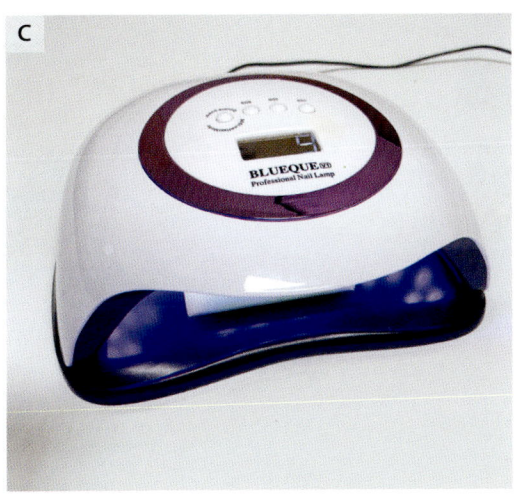

8. Check the edges of the flower for sharp areas. Use a nail file or sandpaper to gently smooth them (**D**).

9. Dab a thin coat of resin on the filed areas (**E**) and cure again.

10. Repeat Steps 1–9 with the second flower to make a matching pair, ensuring consistency in size and coverage.

11. Once they are fully cured, place each flower on the stiff foam block or cushion. Use a handheld jewelry drill to make a small hole near the top of each one, about 3mm from the edge.

12. Brush off any dust that has been generated from the drilling using a powder brush (**F**).

13. Insert a jump ring through each hole, then attach an ear hook to each jump ring using jewelry pliers (**G**).

Project 3:
Fig earrings

These earrings are fun and playful, made with freeze-dried quarter figs that retain a delicate 3D shape while remaining incredibly lightweight. The soft pink and green hues create a charming, eye-catching contrast, and a small crystal adds just the right touch of sparkle. Perfect for casual outfits or occasions where you want a cheerful accessory that draws attention and sparks conversation.

You will need

- ❀ Two freeze-dried fig quarters
- ❀ Silicone block
- ❀ UV resin
- ❀ Plastic rod, toothpick, or needle
- ❀ UV lamp
- ❀ Handheld UV pen
- ❀ Tailor's awl
- ❀ Jewelry pliers (flat nose)
- ❀ Tweezers
- ❀ Jewelry findings (two 4 x 8mm screw eye pins, two 0.7 x 6mm jump rings, two ear hooks all in gold-plated stainless steel)
- ❀ Two boxwood leaves
- ❀ Two 4mm flat-backed Swarovski crystals

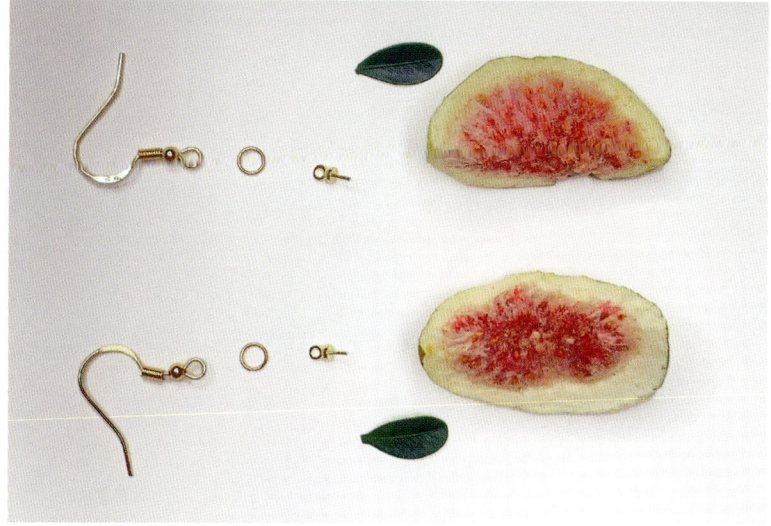

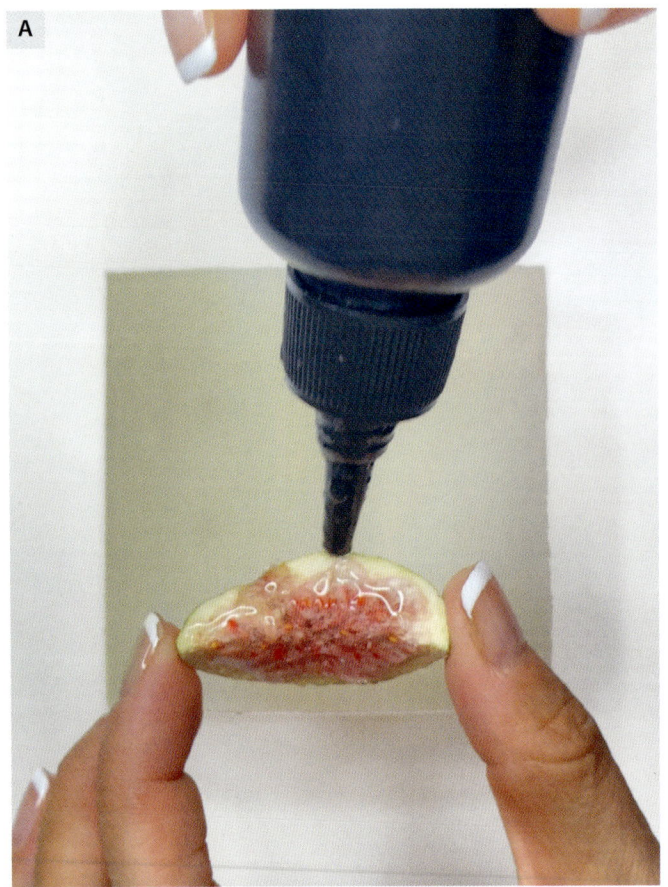

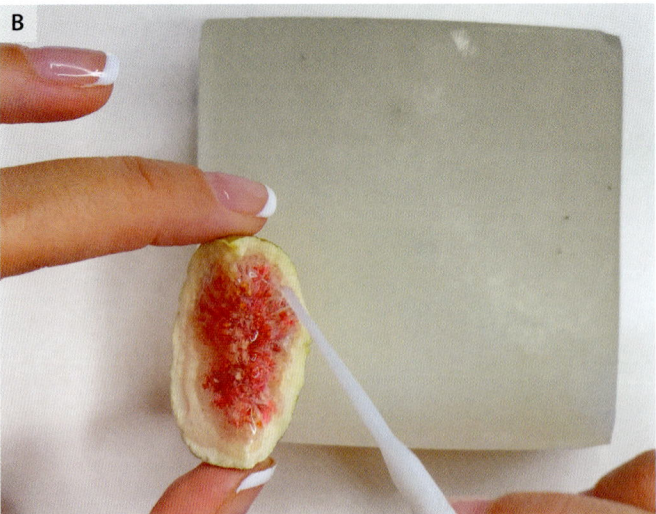

1. Place the fig quarter on a silicone block.

2. Apply a thin layer of UV resin to the inner side of the fig, leaving the top uncovered for attaching a screw eye pin later (A).

3. Use a plastic rod, toothpick, or needle to spread the resin evenly (B).

4. Rotate the fig gently to coat it uniformly (C).

5. Use a handheld UV pen to partially solidify the resin, then cure the resin-coated fig under a UV lamp for 2 minutes.

6. Use a tailor's awl to make a small hole in the uncoated top of the fig.

7. Apply some UV resin to the threaded end of a screw eye pin and insert it into the hole, securing it with jewelry pliers (D).

8. Use a handheld UV light to secure the pin in place, then cure it under the UV lamp for another 2 minutes.

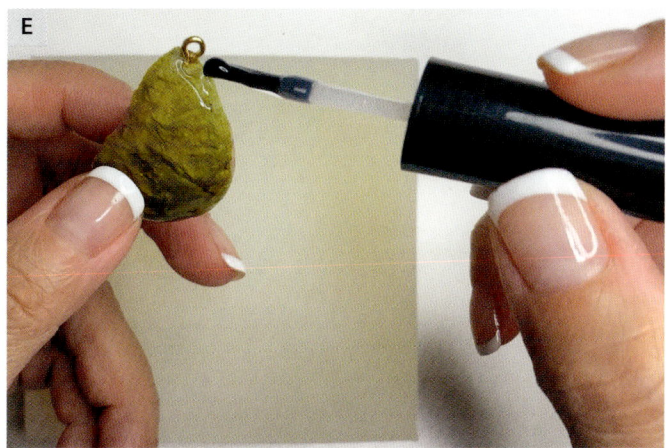

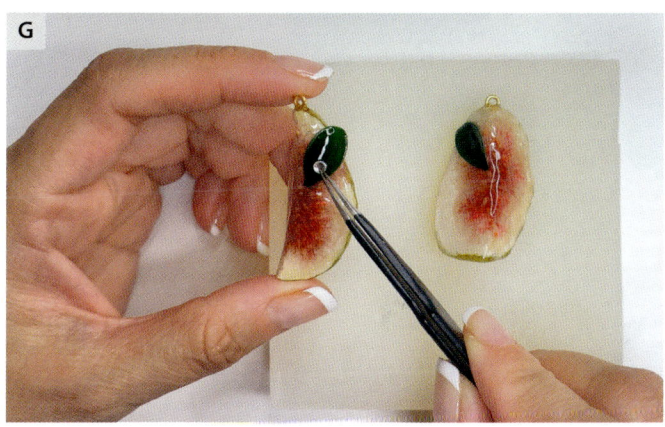

9. Apply a thin coat of UV resin to the outer side of the fig (E). Again, spread the resin evenly with a plastic rod or by rotating the fig.

10. Cure under the UV lamp for 2 minutes. Repeat this coating and curing process as needed until the surface is smooth and fully sealed.

11. Coat both sides of a preserved boxwood leaf with UV resin and cure each side.

12. Use a dot of UV resin to glue the leaf to one side of the inner fig surface and cure to secure the leaf in place (F).

13. Use UV resin and tweezers to glue a Swarovski crystal on top of the leaf, near the stem, and cure (G).

14. Repeat the full process with a second fig to create a matching pair.

15. Once both pieces are fully cured and assembled, insert a jump ring through each eye pin. Attach an ear hook to each earring using jewelry pliers (H).

Project 4:

White hydrangea pearl earrings

Hydrangea forever flowers capture even the tiniest details of each bloom. The white hydrangea highlights the natural vein of the flower, giving the earrings a sense of graceful movement. The petals are delicate and small, so handle them gently to avoid breaking them. Resin helps preserve the flowers and makes them durable while maintaining an elegant, airy appearance. Use minimal resin at first to avoid over curling due to heat generated. Once set, the resin will protect the flower and make the piece durable while keeping its light, airy, and playful elegance. Perfect for formal occasions, these earrings pair beautifully with an elegant dress, offering a look that is light, playful, and refined.

You will need

- ✿ White hydrangea forever flowers: two small and two large
- ✿ Silicone block
- ✿ UV resin
- ✿ Plastic rod, toothpick, or needle
- ✿ UV lamp
- ✿ Stick or tweezers
- ✿ Handheld UV pen
- ✿ Small handheld jewelry drill
- ✿ Stiff foam block or cushion for drilling
- ✿ Powder brush
- ✿ Jewelry pliers (flat nose)
- ✿ Jewelry findings (six 0.7 x 5mm jump rings, two ear hooks, two ¾in- (2cm)-long cable chains all in gold-plated stainless steel)
- ✿ Six 2mm decorative pearls
- ✿ Two 5mm freshwater pearls with bails

1. Place two small and two large white hydrangea forever flowers on a silicone block.

2. Apply a thin layer of UV resin to the top side of each flower (**A**).

3. Use a plastic rod, toothpick, or needle to spread the UV resin evenly (**B**).

4. Cure under a UV lamp for 2 minutes.

5. Once the top is cured, flip each flower over and repeat the process on the back.

6. Coat the front of each large flower with UV resin. Place a smaller flower on top of each larger one with a 45-degree rotation.

A

B

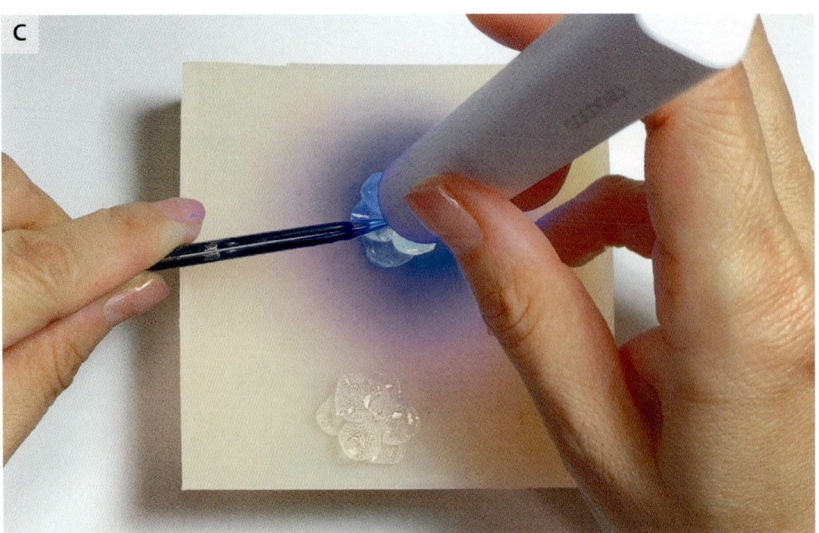

7. Use a stick or tweezers to gently press the two layers together while applying a handheld UV pen for 30 seconds (C). Cure under a UV lamp for another 2 minutes.

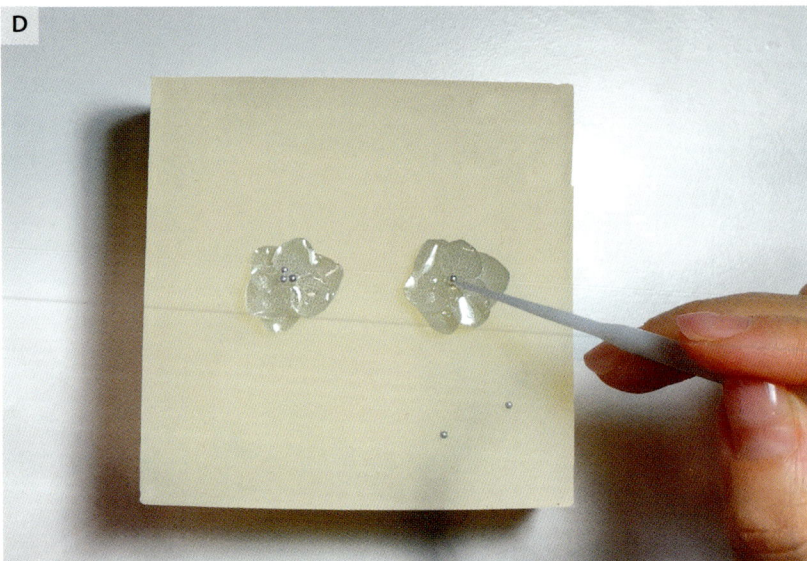

8. Apply a thin droplet of resin in the center of the top flower and add three 2mm pearls to form the flower center. Cure under UV light for 2 minutes (D).

9. Drill a small hole through a petal on each stacked flower, placed on a stiff foam block or cushion (E). Gently remove any dust using a soft powder brush.

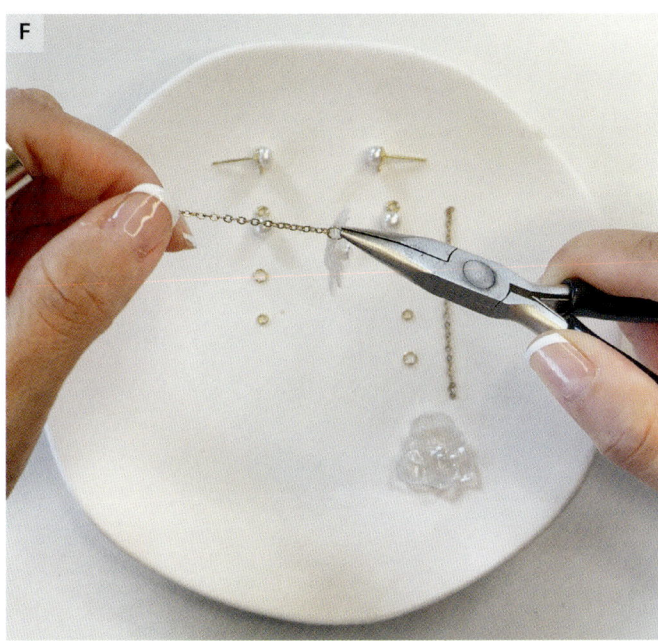

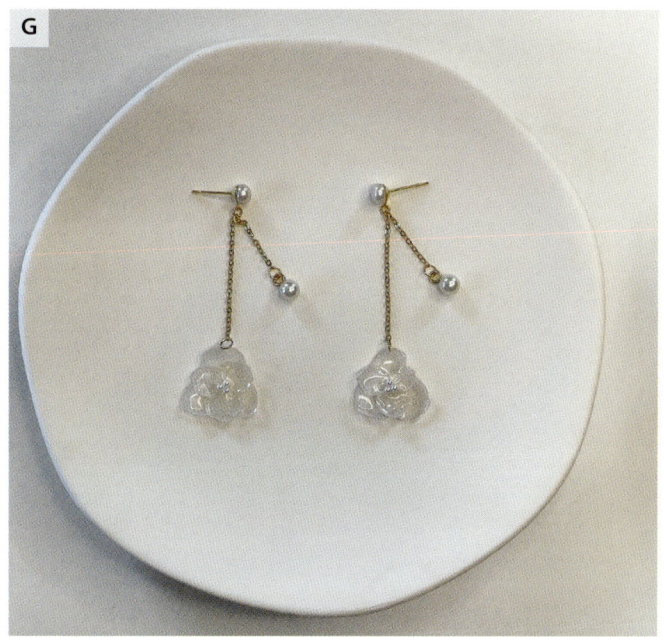

10. Use a jump ring to attach the pressed flower to one end of the chain, and another jump ring to secure a pearl to the opposite end (**F**).

11. About two-thirds to three-quarters along the chain's length, insert a third jump ring and connect it to the ear post. This way, when worn, the flower will dangle slightly lower than the pearl, creating an elegant layered effect (**G**).

Project 5:

Pink marble carnation earrings

These earrings feature delicate pink carnations with a soft marble-like effect, creating a romantic and elegant statement. Carnations are moderately thick flowers, so when pressing these half carnation flowers, remove a few petals and refresh the absorbent plate around day three to ensure even drying. The subtle pink tones and intricate petal textures make these earrings perfect for both casual and semi-formal occasions, adding a gentle, eye-catching touch to any outfit.

You will need

- ✿ Two pressed pink marble carnation flowers
- ✿ Silicone block
- ✿ UV resin
- ✿ Plastic rod, toothpick, or needle
- ✿ UV lamp
- ✿ Small handheld jewelry drill
- ✿ Stiff foam block or cushion for drilling
- ✿ Powder brush
- ✿ Jewelry pliers (flat nose)
- ✿ Jewelry findings (two 3in (80mm) earring threads, two 0.7 x 5mm jump rings all in sterling silver)
- ✿ Two 5mm freshwater pearl pendants (made with peg bail and pearls)

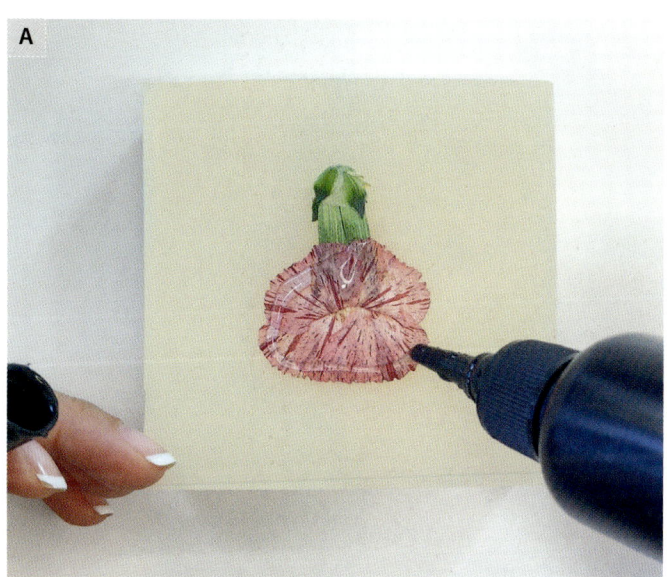

1. Place a flower on a silicone block and apply a thin layer of UV resin to the top side (A).

2. Use a plastic rod to spread the resin evenly across the surface of the flower (B). Cure under a UV lamp for 2 minutes.

3. Once cured, flip the flower over and repeat the process on the back (C).

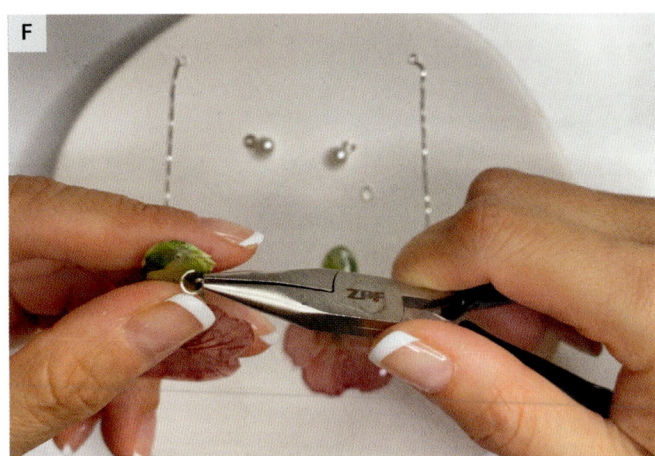

4. Use a nail polish brush to coat the edges of the flower with resin and cure again.

5. Place the flower on a stiff foam block or cushion and drill a small hole through the green stem (**D**).

6. Gently dust off any debris with a powder brush (**E**).

7. Repeat Steps 1–6 with a second flower to form a matching pair.

8. Use jewelry pliers to insert a jump ring through each drilled hole (**F**).

9. Attach a pearl pendant and an ear thread to each jump ring (**G**), then close the ring securely.

Project 6:

Purple primrose earrings

These statement earrings feature deep purple primrose blooms paired with a natural purple crystal, creating a sense of mystery and elegance. The large size makes them a bold, eye-catching accessory, perfect for adding a unique touch to more mature or sophisticated outfits. Pressed primrose flowers are very thin and fragile, so handle them with care to preserve their delicate petals. These earrings are ideal for evening events or occasions where you want a striking, unforgettable piece.

You will need

- ✿ Two pressed purple primrose flowers
- ✿ Silicone block
- ✿ UV resin
- ✿ Plastic rod, toothpick, or needle
- ✿ UV lamp
- ✿ Small handheld jewelry drill

- ✿ Stiff foam block or cushion for drilling
- ✿ Powder brush
- ✿ Jewelry pliers (flat nose)
- ✿ Jewelry findings (four 0.7 x 5mm jump rings, two ear hooks all in gold-plated stainless steel)
- ✿ Wire-wrapped 10mm amethyst crystals

1. Place the first flower on a silicone block and pick a side to begin with.

2. Apply a thin layer of UV resin (**A**).

3. Spread the UV resin evenly using a plastic rod, toothpick, or needle (**B**). Cure the resin under a UV lamp for 2 minutes.

4. Apply a second thin coat of UV resin and cure again for 2 minutes.

5. Turn the flower over and repeat the same resin application and curing steps for the back.

6. Inspect both sides for any uneven or thin areas. Add a small amount of resin where needed and cure for 2 minutes.

7. Use a nail polish brush to coat the edges of the flower with UV resin and cure once more.

8. Once the flower is fully cured, place on a stiff foam block or cushion and drill a small hole about 3mm from the top edge (**C**). Drill another hole near the bottom edge for attaching a dangling crystal. Use a powder brush to remove any dust from drilling.

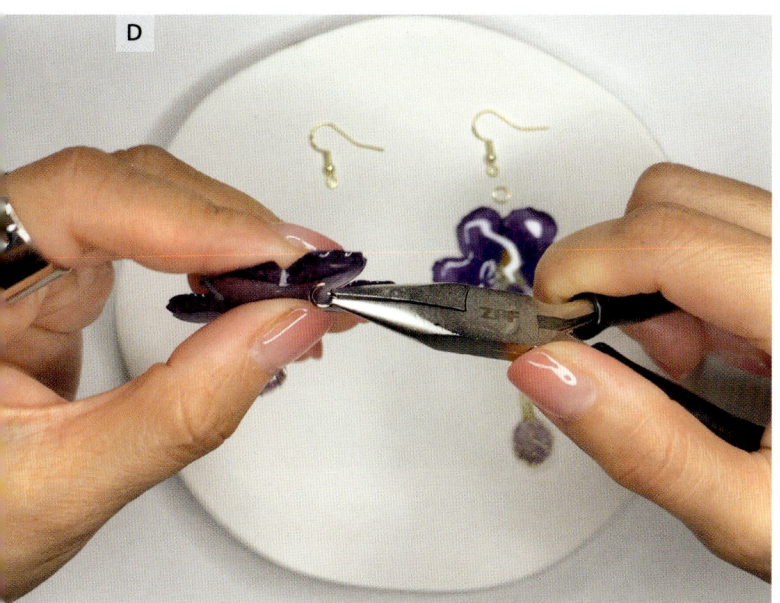

9. Repeat Steps 1–8 to create another flower for the second earring.

10. With jewelry pliers, insert a jump ring into each drilled hole (D).

11. Attach an ear hook to each top jump ring (E).

12. To finish, connect an amethyst crystal to each bottom jump ring (F).

Project 7:

Red maple necklace

This necklace captures the warm, earthy charm of autumn with three red maple leaves – two smaller leaves flanking a larger one in the center – dangling gracefully to create a nostalgic, retro feel. The vibrant red hues evoke the cozy, wistful mood of fall, making this piece perfect for casual or seasonal outfits that celebrate nature's beauty. Pressed maple leaves are thin and delicate, so handle them gently when setting them in resin to preserve their shape and intricate veins.

You will need

- ✿ Pressed red maple leaves: one large, two small
- ✿ Silicone block
- ✿ UV resin
- ✿ Plastic rod, toothpick, or needle
- ✿ Gold foil shavings
- ✿ Handheld UV pen
- ✿ UV lamp
- ✿ Small handheld jewelry drill
- ✿ Stiff foam block or cushion for drilling
- ✿ Powder brush
- ✿ Jewelry pliers (flat nose)
- ✿ Jewelry findings (three 0.6 x 6mm jump rings in gold-plated stainless steel)
- ✿ Ready-made necklace in gold-plated stainless steel

1. Place the large maple leaf on a silicone block.

2. Using a nail polish brush, apply a thin layer of UV resin as an adhesive (**A**).

3. Use tweezers to gently press gold foil shavings onto the resin-coated surface (**B**).

4. Cure the front side under a handheld UV pen for 1 minute (C).

5. Add another layer of resin over the foil using a squeezy bottle (D).

6. Spread the UV resin out with a plastic rod, toothpick, or needle, and cure for 2 minutes (E).

7. Once the front is set, flip the leaf over and repeat the same process on the back (F), leaving a little excess resin around the stalk for durability and for drillings or finding.

8. After both sides are cured, place the leaf on a stiff foam block or cushion (G). Using a handheld jewelry drill, make a small hole near the stem – about 3mm from the edge. Position the drill vertically and apply gentle pressure until the bit passes through the leaf.

9. Repeat Steps 1–6 for the two smaller leaves.

10. Use jewelry pliers to insert a jump ring through each drilled hole (H).

11. Attach the three leaves to the necklace (I), positioning the largest leaf in the middle.

Project 8:

Blue hydrangea bracelet

This bracelet features delicate light-blue hydrangea petals paired with silver accents, creating a subtle and elegant color contrast. The design feels cool and refreshing, making it a perfect accessory for summer outfits. Using single petals gives the piece a light, airy appearance, and this approach can easily be adapted for earrings or necklaces as well. Handle the hydrangea petals gently, as they are thin and fragile.

You will need

- Blue hydrangea forever flowers: two flowers and one additional petal
- Silicone block
- UV resin
- Plastic rod, toothpick, or needle
- UV lamp
- 3mm decorating pearls
- Small handheld drill

- Stiff foam block or cushion for drilling
- Powder brush
- Jewelry pliers (flat nose)
- Jewelry findings (five 0.6 x 5mm oval jump rings in sterling silver)
- Two 2½in- (6cm)-long 3mm chains (any type) – one attached to a clasp, the other to a 4mm chain extension
- 2in- (5cm)-long 0.8mm cable chain in sterling silver

1. Place the blue hydrangea flowers on a silicone block.

2. Apply a thin layer of UV resin (A).

3. Use a toothpick or needle to spread it evenly across all surfaces (B). Cure under a UV lamp for 2 minutes.

4. Apply a second layer of resin and cure again for 2 minutes.

5. Flip each flower over and repeat the Steps 2–4 on the back (C).

6. Prepare the separate flower petal in the same way.

7. Glue the two hydrangea flowers together using UV resin, rotating the top one by about 45 degrees.

8. Add a small pearl to the center and cure for 2 minutes.

9. Place the stacked hydrangea flower on a stiff foam block or cushion. Drill one hole at the top and another at the bottom. Use a powder brush to remove any dust from the drilling.

10. Use jewelry pliers to insert jump rings through the drilled holes of the flower and attach 3mm chain to each side (D).

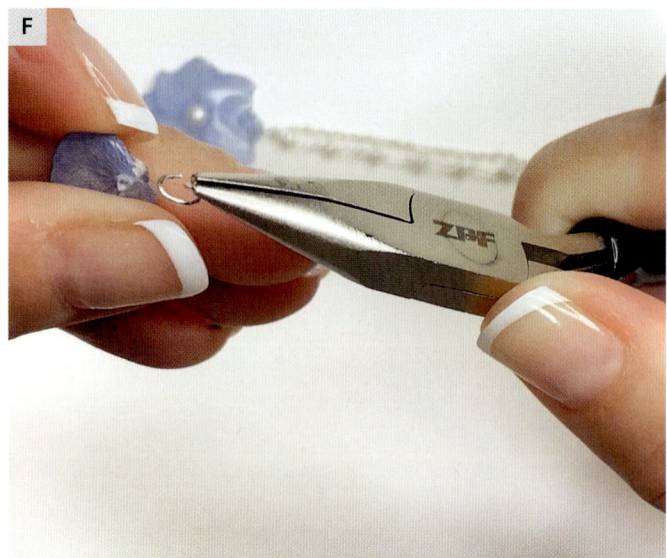

11. On one side, also attach one end of the cable chain (**E**).

12. Use a handheld jewelry drill to create a small hole near the bottom of the resin-coated flower petal. Brush off any debris, then connect the petal to the 0.8mm cable chain in the middle of the chain with a jump ring (**F**).

13. Connect the other end of the cable chain with the main bracelet chain using a jump ring (**G**).

White and purple viola earrings

Viola is a wonderfully versatile flower, offering a range of colors, sizes, and even multi-colored blooms. These earrings feature white and purple violas, carefully dried with silica gel to preserve their delicate 3D shape, adding depth and dimension to the design. To elevate the piece, subtle touches of glitter, mica powder, and other accents give the earrings a luxurious vibe. They are perfect for adding elegance and charm to both casual and semi-formal outfits.

You will need

- Two silica-dried white and purple viola flowers
- Silicone block
- UV resin
- Plastic rod, toothpick, or needle
- UV lamp
- Half-sphere silicone mold
- Fine silver glitter power
- Handheld UV pen
- Jewelry pliers (flat nose)
- Pearls: 20–30 in 2mm and two in 4mm
- Two 6mm-diameter flat pad earring posts in gold-plated stainless steel

1. Place a viola flower on a silicone block. Apply a thin layer of UV resin using a nail polish brush (**A**).

2. Spread the UV resin evenly using a toothpick or needle (**B**). Cure the resin under a UV lamp for 2 minutes.

3. Add UV resin into a half-sphere silicone mold, mix in some silver glitter powder, and dip the tip of a plastic rod into the glitter resin (**C**).

4. Use a plastic rod to apply glitter resin around the outer edges of the flower (**D**).

A

B

C

D

5. Cure the front side under a handheld UV pen for 2 minutes (E).

6. Turn the flower over and repeat the same resin coating and curing steps on the back, without adding glitter (F).

7. Flip the flower face up. Add a 4mm pearl to the center of the flower using a plastic rod (G), then arrange and attach multiple 2mm pearls around it.

8. Use a drop of UV resin to glue a flat pad earring post to the top back of the flower, 4mm from the edge (H).

9. Cure under a handheld UV pen for 2 minutes (I).

10. Repeat Steps 1–9 to create the second earring.

Orange and purple viola ring

As a variation to the white and purple viola earrings, you can create a ring or necklace by choosing the right base and bail. In this example, a metal filigree base is used to support the flower. For extra charm, vary the color of the metal glitter to match the base of the ring, creating a cohesive design. The result is a cute, playful, and beautiful accessory featuring the 3D-shaped viola.

You will need

- One silica-dried orange and purple viola flower
- Silicone block
- UV resin
- Plastic rod, toothpick, or needle
- UV lamp
- Half-sphere silicone mold
- Handheld UV pen
- Pearls: 20–30 in 2mm and two in 4mm

- Fine gold glitter power
- Alcohol wipe
- Metal filigree ring

1. Follow Steps 1–6 for Project 9 to make a resin viola flower. Use fine gold glitter powder in place of the silver glitter used for the earrings.

2. Clean the filigree ring base with an alcohol wipe. Use a nail polish brush to apply a UV resin topcoat to the ring base (**A**).

3. To attach the resin viola flower to the ring base, apply a thin layer of resin to both the ring base and the back of the flower, using resin as the adhesive to bond them together (**B**).

4. Cure under a handheld UV pen for 2 minutes (**C**).

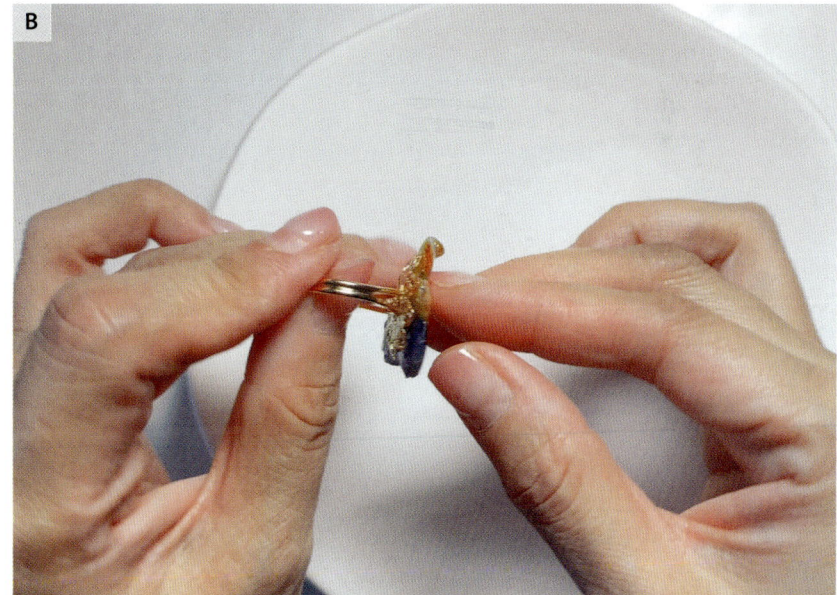

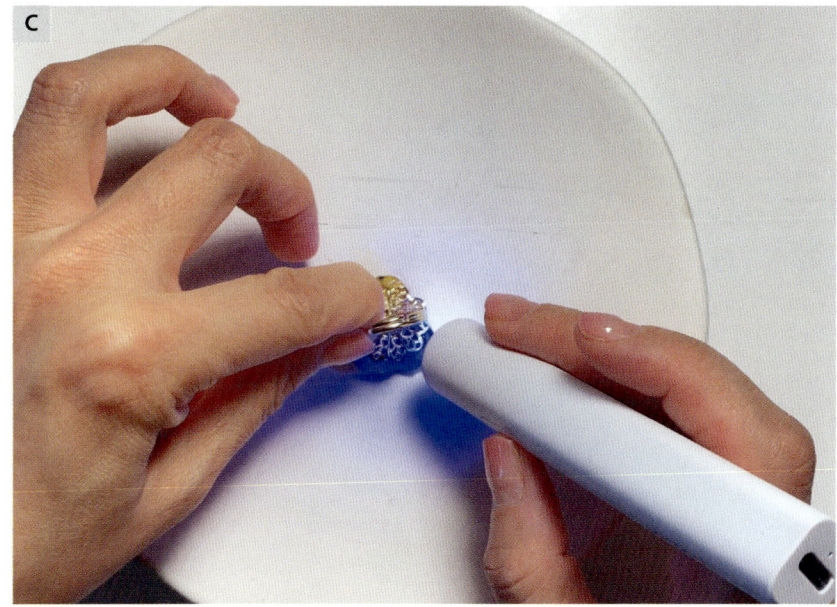

Project 10:

Pink bougainvillea earrings

Bougainvillea is known for its vibrant, fiery color and is a favorite for many flower lovers. Pressed hot-pink bougainvillea holds its color well over time and shows off its distinctive veins with striking clarity. Simply encapsulated in resin, these petals become a bold and beautiful statement piece, allowing their natural brilliance to shine. Perfect for adding a pop of color to your outfit, these earrings celebrate the joyful energy of summer and beyond.

You will need

- ✿ Two silica-dried pink bougainvillea flowers
- ✿ Silicone block
- ✿ UV resin
- ✿ Plastic rod, toothpick, or needle
- ✿ UV lamp
- ✿ Handheld drill
- ✿ Stiff foam block or any cushion for drilling
- ✿ Powder brush
- ✿ Jewelry pliers (flat nose)
- ✿ Jewelry findings (two 0.6 x 6mm jump rings, two ear hooks all in gold-plated stainless steel)

1. Place a bougainvillea flower on a silicone block and apply a thin layer of UV resin (**A**).

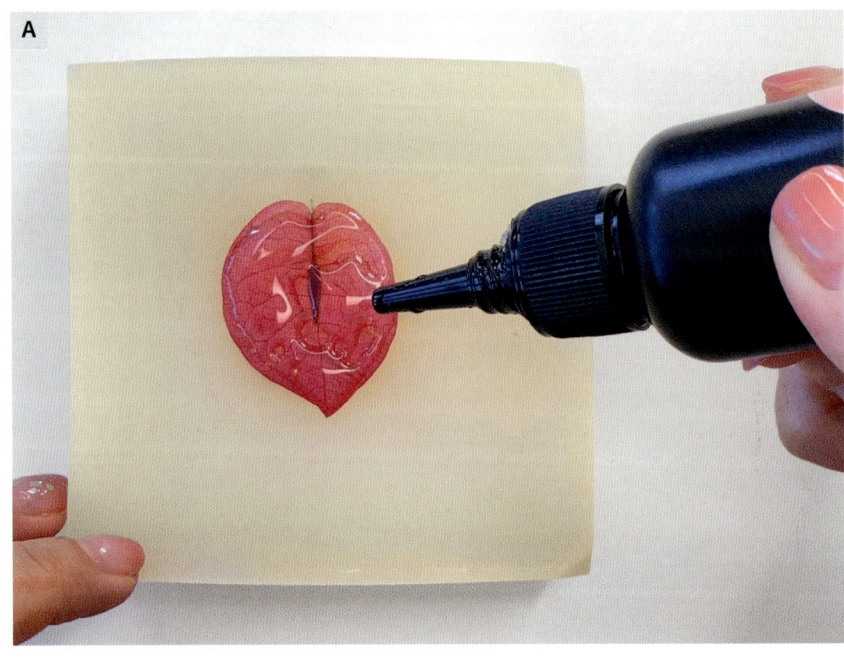

A

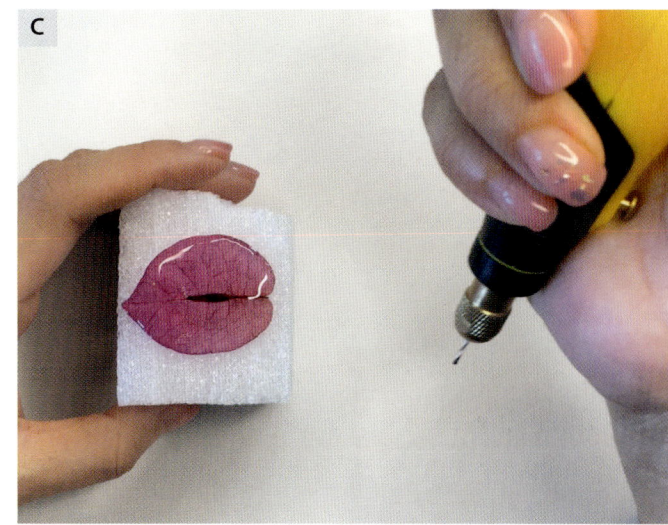

2. Use a plastic rod, toothpick, or needle to spread the UV resin over the flower (B).

3. Cure under UV light for 2 minutes, then apply a second layer of resin and cure again for 2 minutes.

4. Turn the flower over and repeat Steps 1–3 on the back.

5. Once fully cured, use a handheld jewelry drill to make a small hole near the top of the flower, about 3mm from the edge (C).

6. Use a powder brush to remove any dust or debris from the drilling (D).

7. Repeat Steps 1–6 to prepare another flower in the same way.

8. Use jewelry pliers to insert a jump ring through each hole (E).

9. Attach an ear hook to each jump ring to complete the earrings.

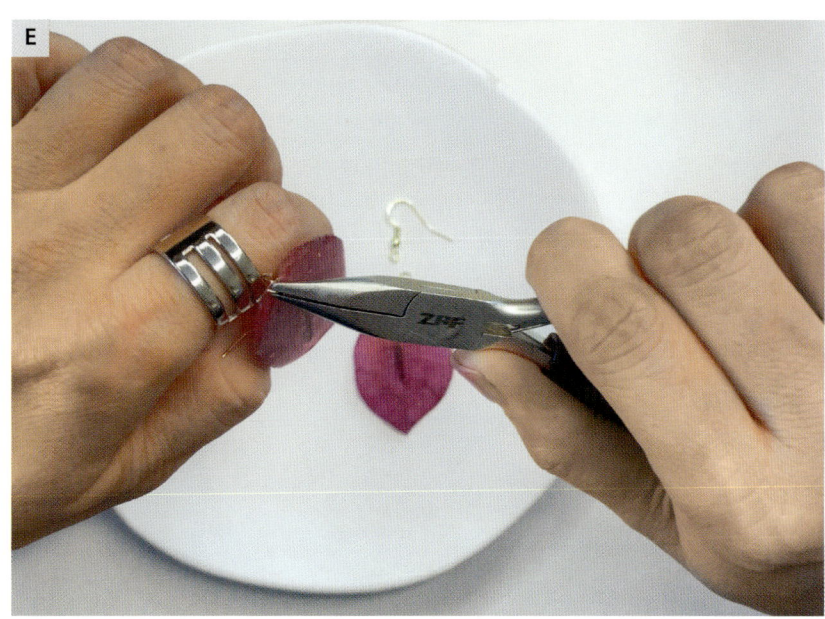

Project 11:

Purple hydrangea frame earrings

Sometimes in jewelry design, adding metal pieces enhances depth and color contrast. In this variation, a diamond-shaped silver frame is introduced as a decorative accent rather than a structural bezel. The encapsulated flower remains the centerpiece, and resin tape is used as a temporary backing for the open frame, allowing the resin to cure cleanly before the frame is added. Unlike the bezel-setting techniques in Chapter 5 (p.93), the frame here serves purely as a design variation, enriching the look while preserving the core encapsulation process.

You will need

- ✿ Four purple hydrangea forever flowers
- ✿ Silicone block
- ✿ UV resin
- ✿ Plastic rod, toothpick, or needle
- ✿ UV lamp
- ✿ Tweezers
- ✿ Two 4mm pearls
- ✿ Handheld UV pen
- ✿ Decorative open pendant bezel
- ✿ Jewelry pliers (flat nose)
- ✿ Resin tape
- ✿ Jewelry findings (two 0.6 x 6mm jump rings, two bowtie stud earrings with a connecting hoop all in sterling silver)

1. Place the purple hydrangea flowers on a silicone block.

2. Apply a thin layer of UV resin using a squeezy bottle, spreading it evenly over the surface (**A**).

3. Use a plastic rod, toothpick, or needle to spread the UV resin over the flower (**B**). Cure under a UV lamp for 2 minutes.

4. Apply a second layer of resin and cure again.

5. Flip the flower and repeat the process on the back.

6. Use tweezers to position two of the cured flowers with a 60-degree rotation between them (**C**).

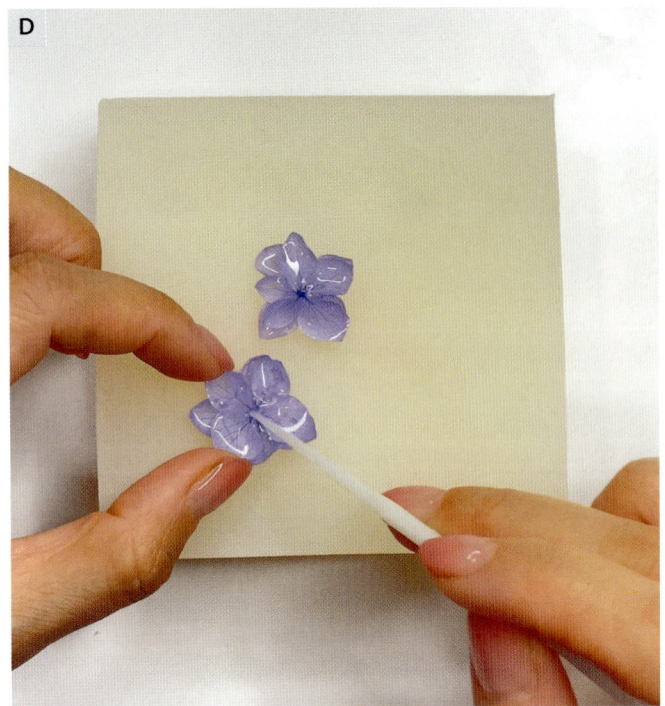

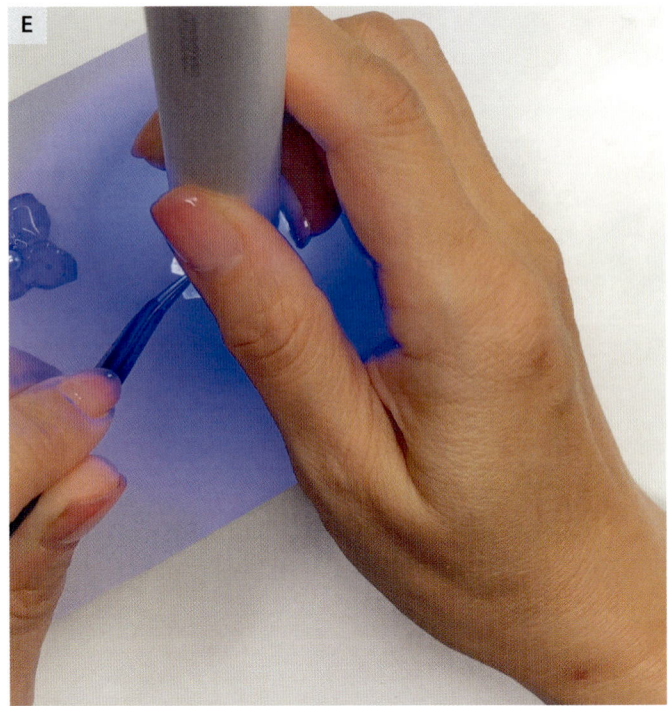

7. Use UV resin to glue the two flowers together (D), then cure under a handheld UV pen for 2 minutes. Repeat for the other two flowers.

8. Use tweezers to add a 4mm pearl at the center of each top flower and cure under a handheld UV pen for 1 minute (E).

9. Cut a piece of resin tape and place it sticky side up on a silicone block. Secure the pendant bezel onto the tape. Fill the bezel with a thin, even layer of UV resin (F).

10. Center the stacked hydrangea flowers inside the resin-filled bezel (G). Cure under a UV lamp for 2 minutes.

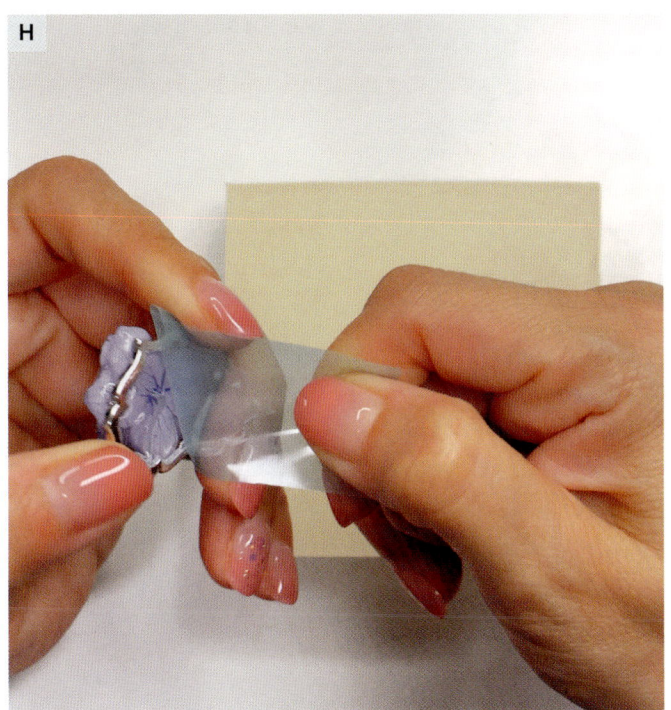

11. Once cured, gently peel off the resin tape from the back of the bezel (H).

12. Repeat Steps 9–11 for the second earring.

13. Use jewelry pliers to insert a jump ring through the loop of each bezel (I).

14. Connect each jump ring to a bowtie stud earring with a connecting hoop (J).

Project 12:

Hydrangea multiple flower earrings

Once you feel comfortable working with single flowers, you can start experimenting by combining petals to "construct" new blooms. Hydrangea petals are perfect for this – individual petals can be separated and reassembled into a larger flower shape, with a small bloom placed at the center as the flower core to create a lotus-like effect. You can also mix and match different colors for playful or dramatic results, giving each piece a unique and creative character.

You will need

- ❀ Purple hydrangea forever flowers: four darker purple flowers, two smaller purple flowers, two white flowers
- ❀ Silicone block
- ❀ UV resin
- ❀ Plastic rod, toothpick, or needle
- ❀ UV lamp
- ❀ Tweezers
- ❀ Stiff foam block or any cushion for drilling
- ❀ Handheld drill
- ❀ Powder brush
- ❀ Two irregular-shaped round hoops (40mm diameter)
- ❀ Jewelry pliers (flat nose)
- ❀ Jewelry findings (two round head stud earrings with ring, six 0.7 x 6mm jump rings all in gold-plated stainless steel)

1. Place the purple hydrangea forever flowers on a silicone block.

2. Apply a thin layer of UV resin on each flower. Use a plastic rod, toothpick, or needle to spread the UV resin over each flower. Cure under a UV lamp for 2 minutes.

3. Apply a second layer of resin and cure again. Flip the flower and repeat the process on the back.

4. Position two of the larger cured flowers with a 60-degree rotation between them. Use UV resin to glue the two flowers together, then cure for 2 minutes.

5. Repeat the process to add a smaller hydrangea flower on top (**A**).

6. Use a drop of UV resin and tweezers to glue the white flower onto the flower stack (**B**). Cure under a UV lamp for 2 minutes.

7. Use a handheld jewelry drill to make a small hole on one petal of the bottom purple hydrangea flower, approximately 3mm from the edge (**C**). Use a powder brush to remove any dust or debris from the drilling.

8. Repeat Steps 1–7 to make a second earring. (D).

9. Use jewelry pliers to insert a jump ring through the drilled hole in each flower (E).

10. Insert another jump ring through the hoop (F) and a third jump ring through the loop of each stud earring.

11. Connect all three jump rings together on each earring to assemble the final piece (G).

G

Design with Bezels and Frames

In this chapter, we'll explore a new dimension in natural resin flower jewelry – incorporating frames and bezels as design elements. These components add structure and depth, allowing for layer-by-layer compositions that combine various flowers with embellishments such as gold and silver gravel. When working with a thin bezel but aiming to create a 3D multilayer effect, add elements to the back.

Frames and bezels come in a variety of shapes, sizes, and depths. Choose one that complements your design vision and fits the size of your floral and decorative elements. Some bezels have built-in loops for jump rings, making jewelry assembly easy. If your bezel doesn't have loops, you can still turn it into a wearable piece by drilling a hole in the cured resin for a jump ring, drilling a vertical hole and using a peg bail, or attaching a glue-on bail to the back of the piece.

Before starting any project, always clean your frames and bezels with an alcohol wipe or a cotton swab soaked with alcohol to remove dust, oils, or residue that might interfere with resin adhesion and the final finish. When working with larger frames, be sure to build your resin in thin layers. Thicker pours can lead to uneven curing, curling, or warping. Layering slowly ensures a smooth, stable, and polished result.

Using resin tape

A key material introduced in this chapter is resin tape – a no-residue adhesive tape (often light blue) commonly available at craft stores or online. You can find it by searching for "resin tape" or "bezel tape" on platforms like Etsy and Amazon. Resin tape acts as a temporary backing for open frames or bezels, letting you pour and build your resin directly onto it. Once the resin cures, simply peel away the tape to reveal a clean-backed piece.

To create a tight, leak-proof seal between the tape and the frame, use a pen or pencil with a soft rubber grip to gently press and roll the frame down against the tape on a silicone block. This ensures resin doesn't seep underneath during curing.

These tapes are designed to leave minimal residue. However, occasionally, residue may remain on the bezel or resin. In such cases, simply press a fresh piece of tape repeatedly onto the sticky area to lift it off.

After removing the tape, the back of the resin piece may not always be smooth due to tape marks. To achieve a smooth, glossy finish, apply a very thin layer of UV resin and cure it. If you prefer a three-dimensional look, you can apply a thicker layer to create a dome effect, like the front. It all depends on your personal preference.

Project 13:

Fleabane daisy earrings

Fleabane daisies are common wildflowers that bloom abundantly in spring. Most are bright white, though some have delicate pink edges, making them the first cheerful messengers of the season. Their needle-like petals are intricate and beautiful, adding a natural delicacy to jewelry designs. In this project, the fleabane is set within frames and paired with blue-colored resin, creating a vivid background that makes the flower's details stand out.

You will need

- ✿ Round open-back pendant bezel (1in/25mm in diameter)
- ✿ Alcohol wipe
- ✿ Resin tape
- ✿ Silicone block
- ✿ Soft-gripped pen
- ✿ Small semi-sphere silicone mold
- ✿ UV resin
- ✿ Transparent blue alcohol ink
- ✿ Tweezers
- ✿ Two pressed white fleabane daisy flowers
- ✿ Plastic rod, toothpick, or needle
- ✿ UV lamp
- ✿ Jewelry pliers (flat nose)
- ✿ Jewelry findings (two 0.7 x 5mm jump rings, two ready-made post earrings with loops all in gold-plated stainless steel)

1. Thoroughly clean the bezel with an alcohol wipe before applying resin to ensure proper adhesion.

2. Cut a piece of resin tape and place it sticky side up on a silicone block. Press the pendant bezel firmly onto the tape (**A**). Use a soft-gripped pen to rub the bezel gently back and forth, ensuring a tight seal between the tape and bezel.

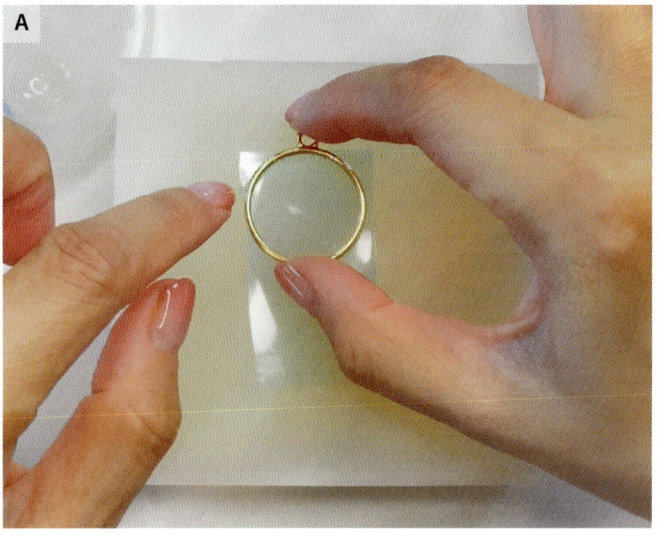

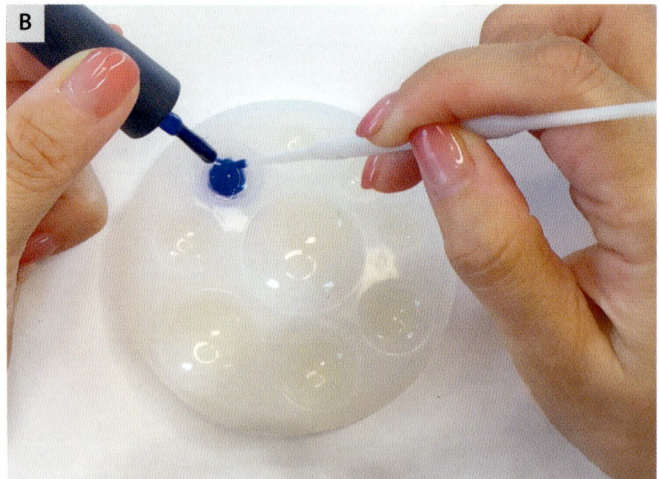

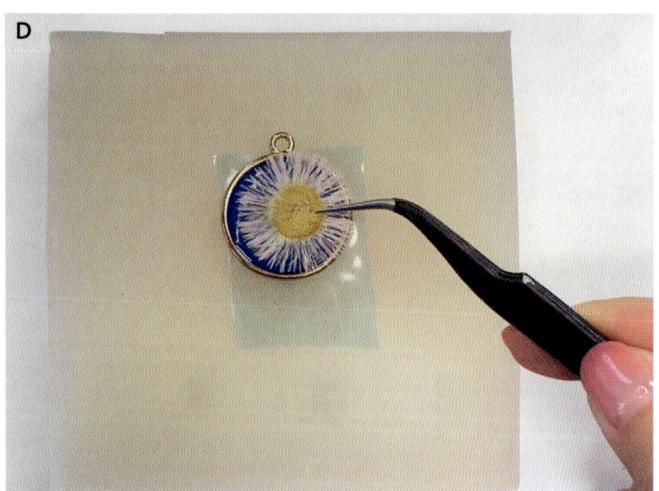

3. In a small semi-sphere silicone mold, add approximately 3ml (around 10 drops) of UV resin and half a drop of blue alcohol ink. Mix them gently and thoroughly using a plastic rod, toothpick, or needle (**B**).

4. Add the blue resin into the bezel with a plastic rod, forming a thin, even base (**C**). Remove any air bubbles.

5. Use tweezers to place the fleabane daisy flower face up in the resin (**D**). Cure under a UV lamp for 2 minutes.

6. Add a second layer of clear UV resin on top, slightly overfilling to create a subtle dome (**E**). Cure for 2 minutes.

7. Carefully peel the resin tape from the back (**F**).

G

H

L

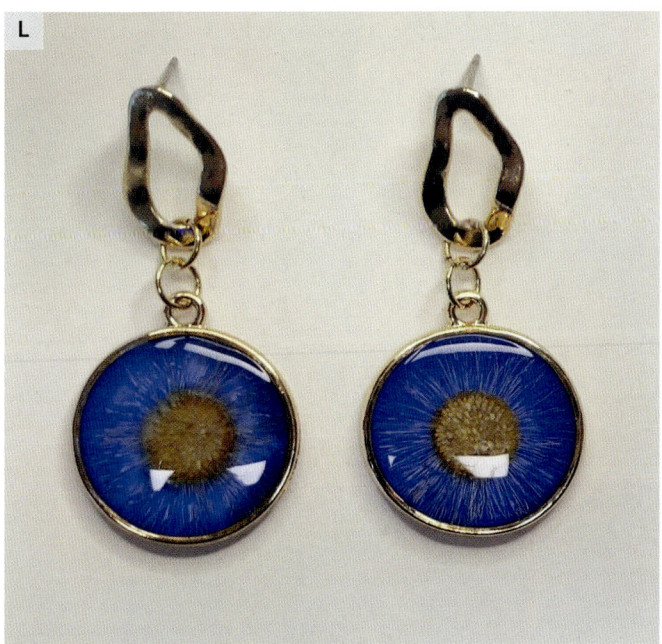

8. To smooth out any marks, apply a thin layer of UV resin to the back (**G**) and cure for 2 minutes.

9. Use jewelry pliers to insert a jump ring through the pendant loop.

10. Attach a post earring to each jump ring using jewelry pliers (**H**).

11. Repeat Steps 1–10 to create the second earring (**I**).

Project 14:

Purple lantana necklace

antana flowers are known for their clusters of tiny blooms and vibrant colors, often blending several shades in a single cluster. This necklace highlights the charm of purple lantana, capturing its playful yet elegant look. The clustered petals create natural volume and texture, while gold gravel is added to the design for extra depth and a subtle sparkle. The combination of purple and gold gives the piece a rich, eye-catching character. Perfect as a statement necklace, it pairs beautifully with both casual and dressy outfits.

You will need

- Waterdrop-shaped open-back pendant bezel in gold color
- Alcohol wipe
- Resin tape
- Silicone block
- Soft-gripped pen
- Pressed purple lantana flowers
- Tweezers
- UV resin
- Plastic rod or toothpick
- UV lamp
- Gold foil shavings or gravel
- Jewelry pliers (flat nose)
- Jewelry findings (0.7 x 5mm jump ring, 16–18in (41–46cm) adjustable cable chain necklace all in gold-plated stainless steel)

1. Clean the bezel thoroughly with an alcohol wipe.

2. Cut a piece of resin tape and place it sticky side up on a silicone block. Place the pendant bezel onto the tape (**A**) and secure it using a soft-gripped pen.

3. Squeeze UV resin into the bezel to form a thin base layer. Remove all air bubbles using a plastic rod or toothpick (**B**).

4. Pull petals from the pressed purple lantana flowers and use tweezers to arrange them as desired in the bezel (**C**).

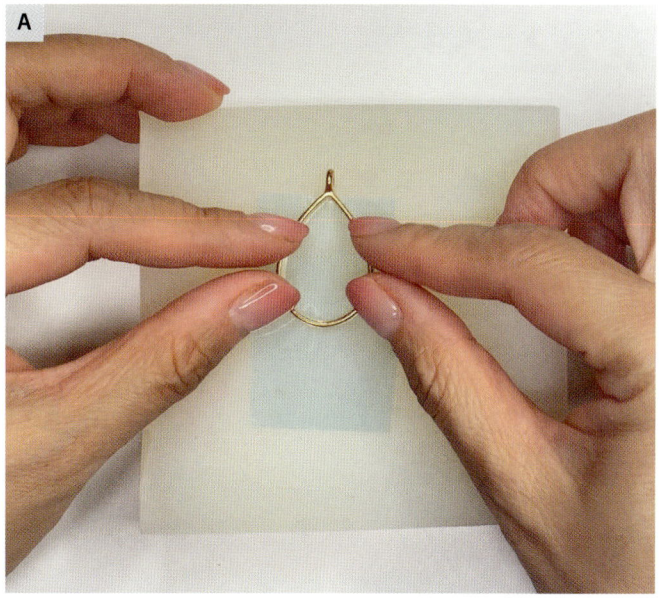

5. Add gold foil shavings or gold gravel for embellishment, using a plastic rod or toothpick to position the pieces (D). Cure under a UV lamp for 2 minutes.

6. Apply a second layer of UV resin on top to create a slight dome (E). Cure under a UV lamp for 2 minutes.

7. Slowly peel the resin tape from the back. To mask tape marks or imperfections, apply a thin coat of UV resin to the back and cure under UV light for 2 minutes.

8. Use jewelry pliers to insert a jump ring through the pendant loop (F).

9. Place the necklace chain inside the jump ring and close it securely to complete the piece (G).

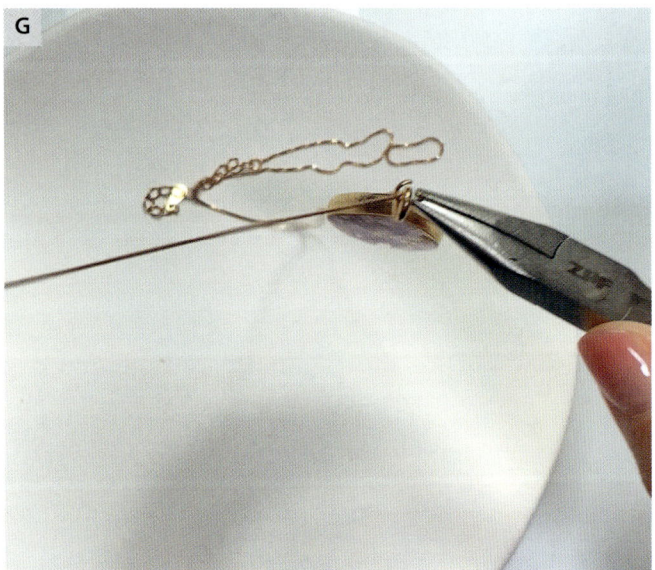

Project 15:

Purple statice, blue cornflower, and orange marigold earrings

This design combines petals from three different flowers – purple statice, blue cornflower, and orange marigold – to create earrings with striking color contrast and visual richness. The bold orange of marigold is balanced by the deep purple tones of statice and the vivid blue of cornflower, resulting in a lively and harmonious palette. By mixing petals, you can achieve a unique layered effect, adding depth and character to your jewelry. These earrings are perfect for anyone who enjoys vibrant accessories that stand out.

You will need

- Round stainless steel frames (1in (25mm) in diameter)
- Alcohol wipe
- Resin tape
- Silicone block
- Soft-gripped pen
- UV resin
- Plastic rod or toothpick
- Dried purple statice flowers, blue cornflowers, and orange marigold flowers
- Tweezers
- Silver foil

- UV lamp
- UV pen
- Scissors
- Handheld drill
- Stiff foam block or cushion for drilling
- Powder brush
- Jewelry pliers (flat nose)
- Jewelry findings (four 0.7 x 5mm jump rings, two French earring hooks all in sterling silver)
- Teardrop-shaped Czech beads in purple/blue (8mm long)

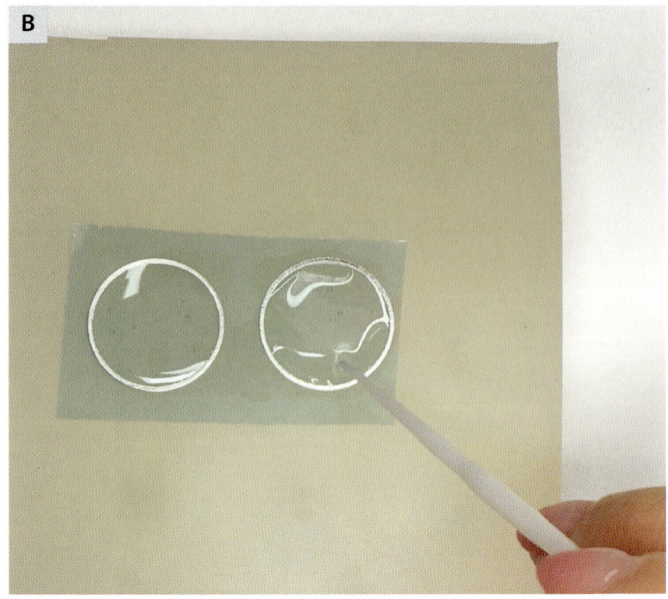

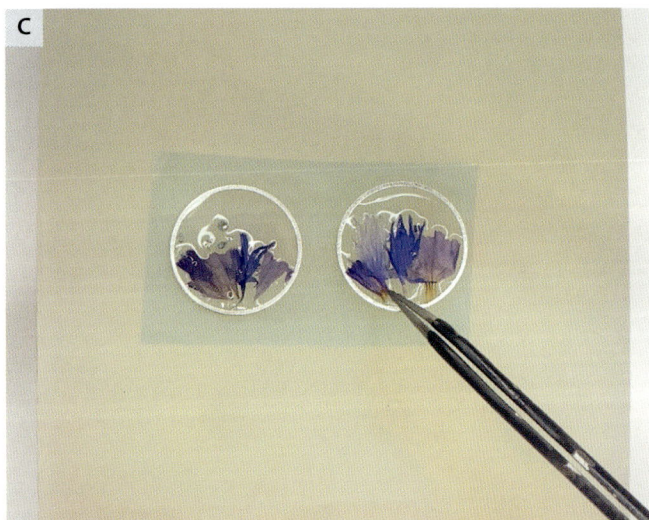

1. Clean the stainless steel frames thoroughly with an alcohol wipe.

2. Cut a piece of resin tape and place it sticky side up on a silicone block. Place the round frames onto the tape and press them down using a soft-gripped pen to secure a tight seal (**A**).

3. Squeeze UV resin into the bezel to form a thin base layer. Remove all air bubbles using a plastic rod or toothpick (**B**).

4. Pull the petals from the purple statice and blue cornflowers and arrange them as desired using tweezers (**C**). Add silver foil to fill the empty spaces. Cure under a UV lamp for 2 minutes.

5. The purple statice and blue cornflowers are air dried, so they have volume. If they stick out of the frame too high, trim them down using scissors (**D**) so the resin can cover them evenly.

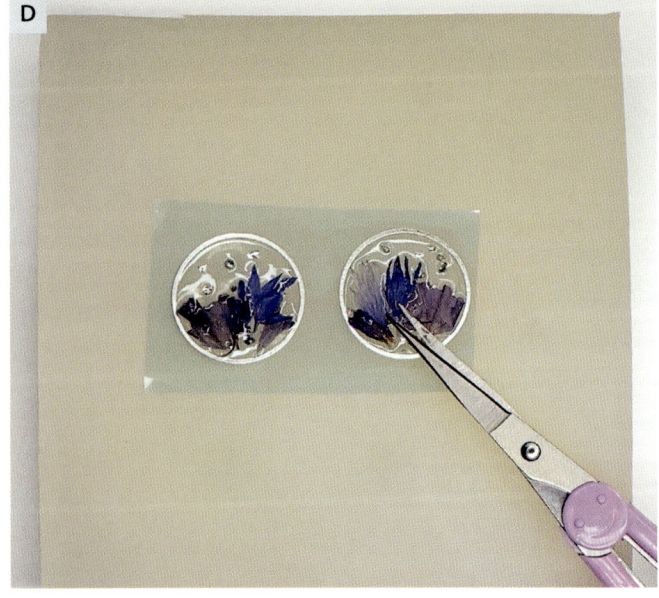

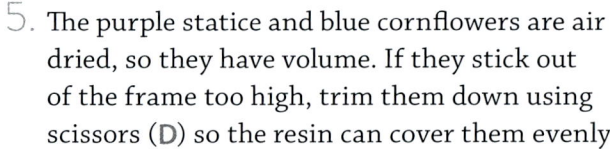

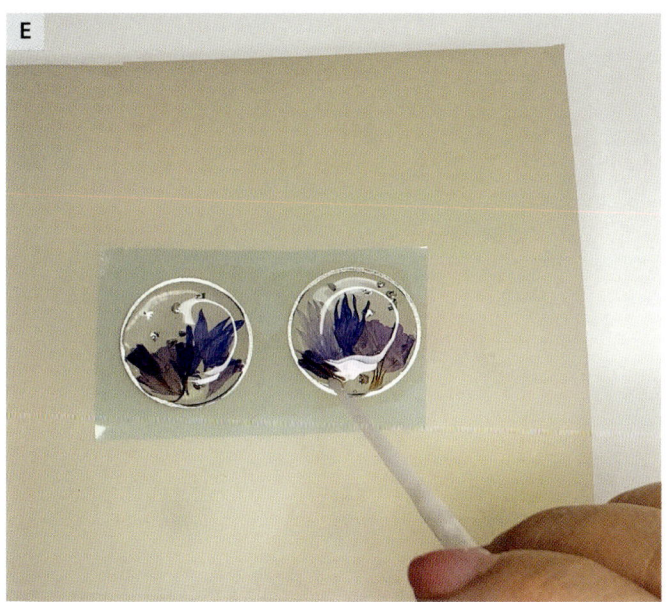

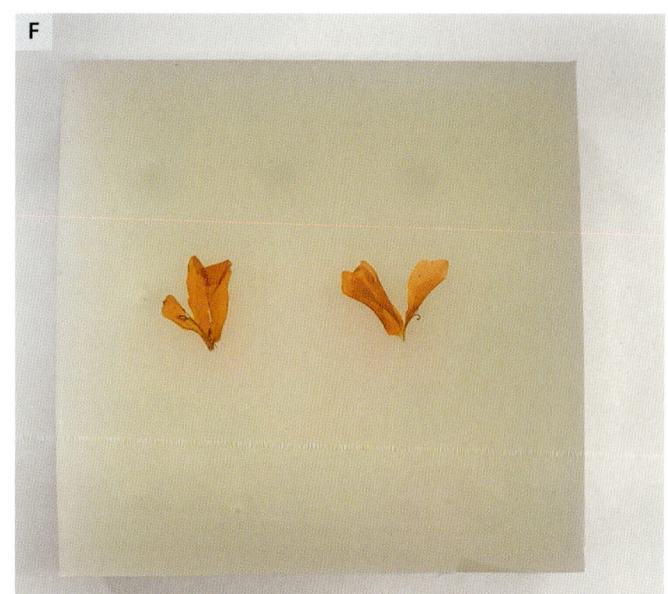

6. Apply a second layer of UV resin on top of the first layer, slightly overfilling to form a dome. Again, remove all air bubbles using a plastic rod or toothpick (E). Cure under a UV lamp for 2 minutes.

7. Slowly peel the resin tape from the back.

8. Arrange marigold petals on the silicone block for the back (F).

9. Apply a thin coat of UV resin to act as an adhesive, then place the bezel face up, with the resin-coated back pressing onto the petal, arranging them in place with tweezers (G).

10. Cure from the top with a handheld UV pen for 1 minute to bond (H).

11. Turn the bezel over and apply a final layer of UV resin to the back (I). Cure for 2 minutes.

12. Once fully cured, place the piece on a small foam block or cushion and drill a small hole near the top, approximately 3mm from the edge (J). Drill another hole near the bottom edge for the Czech bead. Use a powder brush to remove any dust from the drilling.

13. Use one jump ring to attach the Czech bead to the bottom hole drilled in the resin pendant, then use a second jump ring to connect the ear hook to the top hole of the pendant (K).

Project 16:

Purple statice and blue cornflower necklace

This necklace combines delicate purple statice with soft blue cornflower petals, creating a subtle yet striking look. The cool-toned palette makes it a versatile piece that pairs beautifully with both blue- and pink-toned outfits. While the design feels understated, the natural contrast between purple and blue ensures it still catches the eye. Perfect for adding a touch of elegance without overwhelming your style.

You will need

- Half circle gold-plated stainless steel frame (1in (25mm) in diameter)
- Alcohol wipe
- Resin tape
- Silicone block
- Soft-gripped pen
- UV resin
- Plastic rod or toothpick
- Dried purple statice and blue cornflowers
- Tweezers

- Gold gravel
- UV lamp
- Handheld drill
- Stiff foam block or cushion for drilling
- Powder brush
- Jewelry pliers (flat nose and cutting pliers)
- Jewelry findings (two 0.7 x 5mm jump rings, 16–18in (41–46cm) ready-made cable chain all in gold-plated stainless steel)

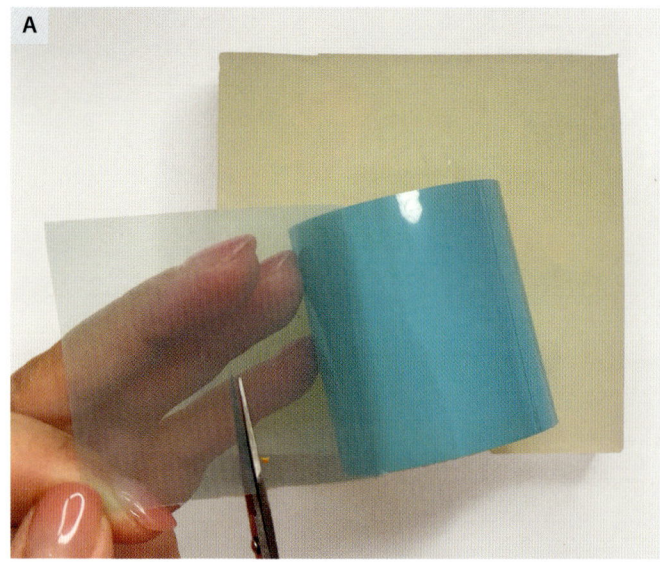

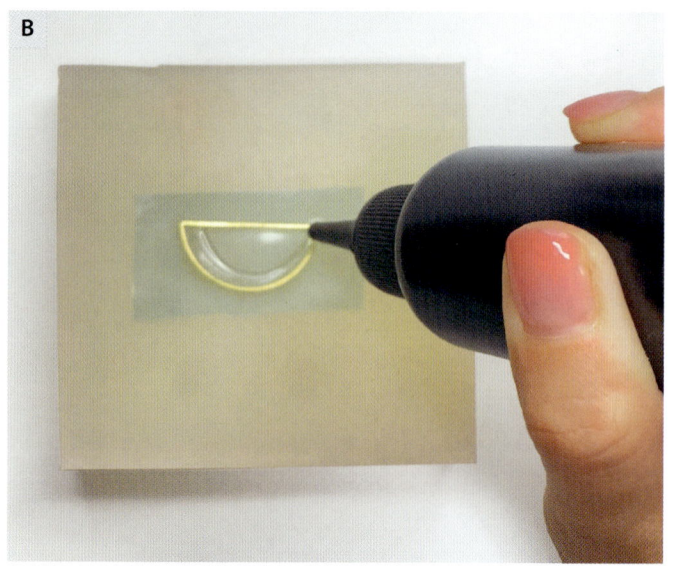

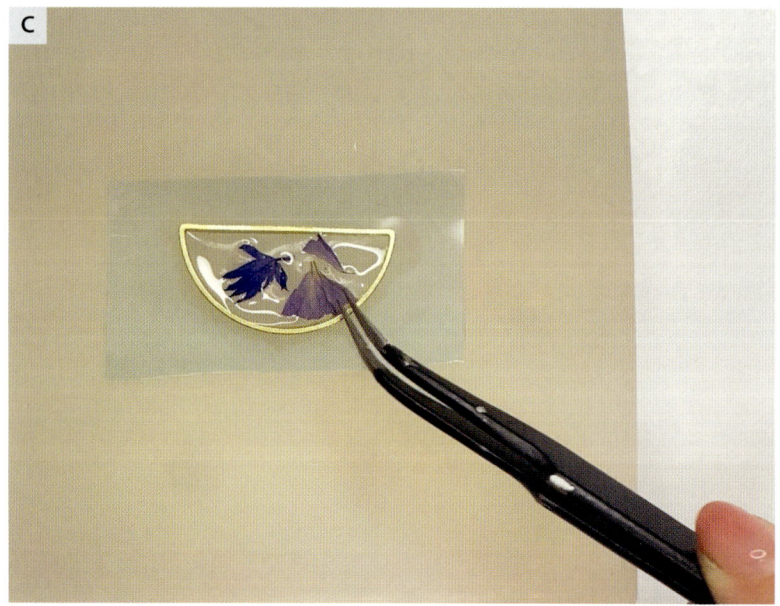

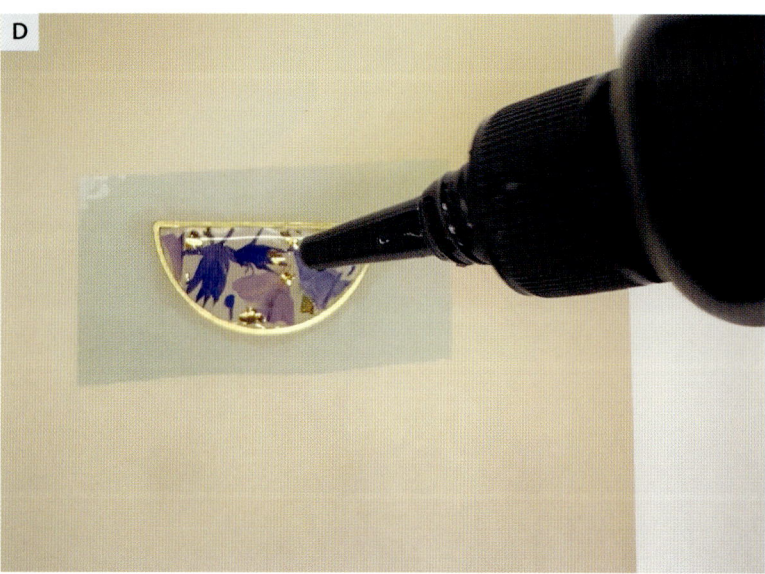

1. Clean the stainless steel frame thoroughly with an alcohol wipe.

2. Cut a piece of resin tape (**A**) and place it sticky side up on a silicone block. Place the half-circle frame onto the tape and press it down with a soft-gripped pen to secure a tight seal.

3. Squeeze UV resin into the bezel to form a thin base layer (**B**). Remove all air bubbles with a plastic rod or toothpick.

4. Pull the petals from the flowers and arrange them with tweezers, as desired (**C**). Add crushed gold gravel to fill the spaces. Cure under a UV lamp for 2 minutes.

5. Apply a second layer of UV resin to form a slight dome over the surface (**D**). Cure under a UV lamp for another 2 minutes.

E

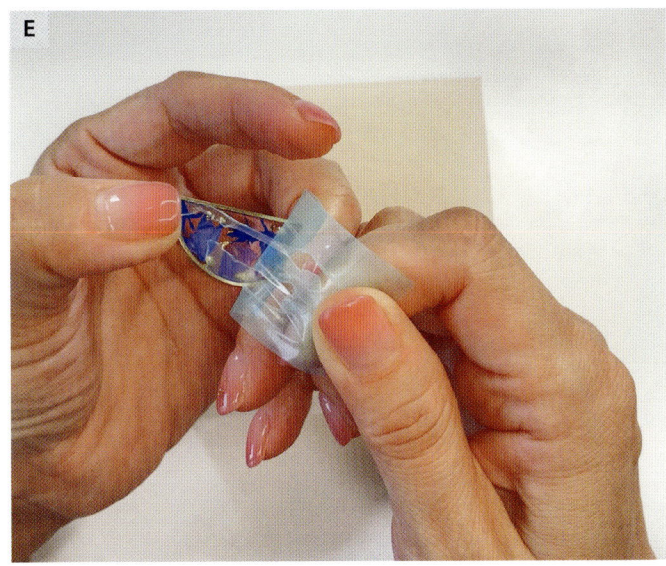

F

6. Carefully peel the resin tape from the back of the bezel (**E**).

7. Apply a thin coat of UV resin to the back to mask any tape marks or imperfections, then cure under UV light for 2 minutes.

8. Once fully cured, use a handheld jewelry drill to make two small holes near the top left and right corners of the pendant, about 3mm from each edge (**F**). These will be used to attach the chain.

9. Cut a ready-made cable chain in half using cutting pliers. Insert a jump ring through the top left hole and one end of the chain. Close the jump ring to secure the connection (**G**).

10. Repeat on the top right side with the other half of the necklace to finish.

G

Purple and orange viola earrings

Crafted with multicolored viola petals, these earrings feature a warm and rich color palette of deep purple and vibrant orange. The combination brings a retro charm and an oil painting-like texture, making them feel both artistic and timeless. Great for pairing with warm-toned, semi-formal outfits, they add just the right touch of elegance and personality.

You will need

- Two round open bezels (¾in (20mm) in diameter)
- Alcohol wipe and mild soap
- Silicone block
- Dried yellow and purple viola flowers
- UV resin
- Plastic rod or toothpick
- UV lamp
- UV pen

- Jewelry pliers (flat nose and cutting pliers)
- Jewelry findings (two 6mm flat pad earring posts, two 5mm pearls with 3 x 6.9mm peg bails all in gold-plated stainless steel)
- Sandpaper (optional)
- Handheld drill
- Stiff foam block or cushion for drilling
- Powder brush
- Tweezers

A

B

C

1. Clean the bezels thoroughly with an alcohol wipe.

2. Place the bezel onto the front surface of the flowers on a silicone block (**A**).

3. Squeeze UV resin into the bezel to form a thin base layer. Remove any air bubbles using a plastic rod or toothpick (**B**). Cure under a UV lamp for 2 minutes.

4. Once the resin has cured, use cutting pliers to trim off any parts of the flowers extending beyond the bezel (**C**).

5. Flip the piece over and apply a thin layer of UV resin to the back of the flower (**D**). Remove any air bubbles using a plastic rod or toothpick and cure again for 2 minutes.

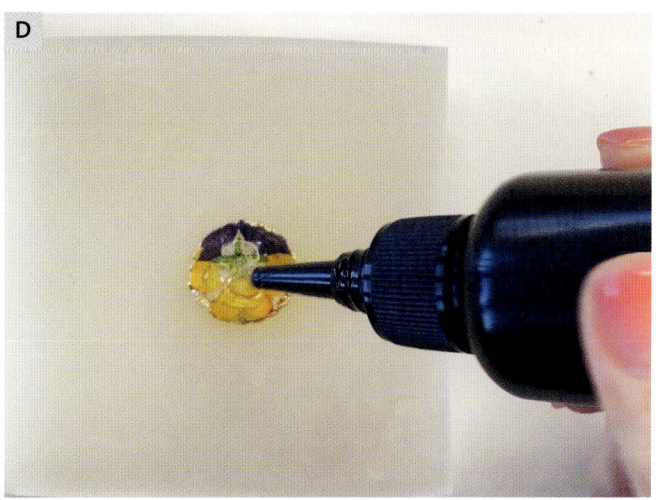

D

6. Add another layer of UV resin to the front of the bezel to level and seal the piece. Repeat the process on the back of the flower to ensure full coverage.

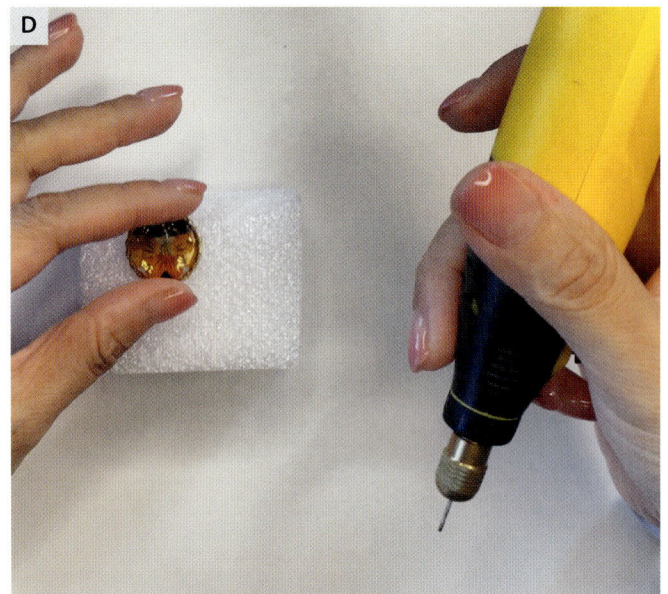

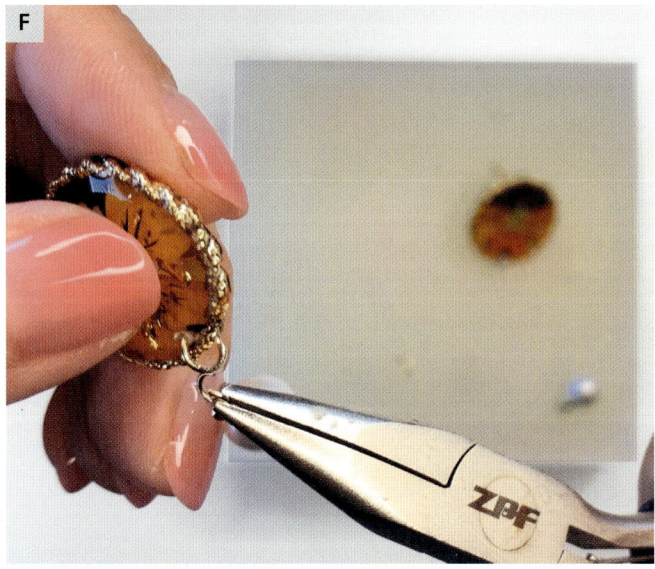

7. To prepare the pearl pendant, use a plastic rod to apply a tiny drop of UV resin into the opening of the pre-drilled pearl. Insert a peg into the hole and hold it steady while curing with a UV pen for 1 minute.

8. Once all resin has cured, drill a small hole near the bottom center of the pendant, about 2mm from the edge (E). This will allow you to attach the jump ring. Use a powder brush to remove any dust or debris from the drilling.

9. Clean the flat pad earring posts with alcohol or mild soap to remove any oils or dust. Optionally, lightly sand the surface for better adhesion. Apply a drop of UV resin to the center back of the pendant, press the pad post into place, and cure under UV light for 2 minutes.

10. Use jewelry pliers to insert a jump ring through the drilled hole and through the peg of the pearl pendant (F).

11. Close the jump ring securely to complete the assembly.

12. Repeat the whole process to create the second earring (G).

Project 18:

Blue lobelia earrings

Lobelia is a delicate, subtle flower with a soft cubic shape. On its own, it carries quiet beauty, so this design highlights it by layering complementary structural elements. A dark blue frame sets the stage, paired with a matching blue stud for balance. Vibrant blue tassels complete the look, drawing the eye while allowing the lobelia to blend in naturally. The result is a harmonious piece where every element flows together – versatile enough to elevate both casual and formal outfits.

You will need

- Two blue square open bezels (³⁄₄ x ³⁄₄in (20 x 20mm))
- Alcohol wipe
- Resin tape
- Silicone block
- UV resin
- Plastic rod or toothpick
- Two pressed blue lobelia flowers
- Tweezers
- UV lamp
- Handheld drill
- Stiff foam block or cushion for drilling
- Powder brush
- Jewelry pliers (flat nose)
- Jewelry findings (two blue triangle earring studs with attached ring, two 0.7 x 6mm jump rings all in gold-plated stainless steel)
- Two blue tassels

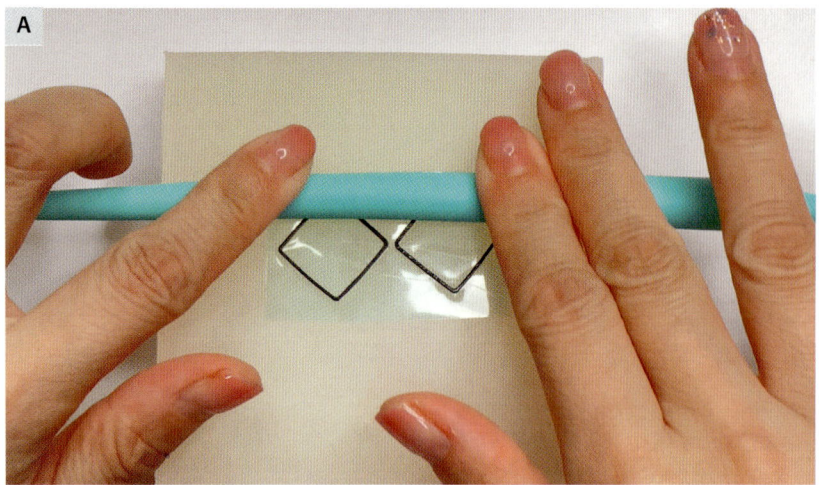

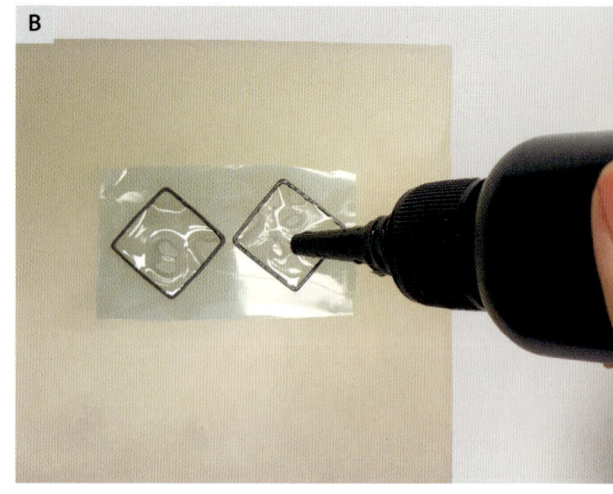

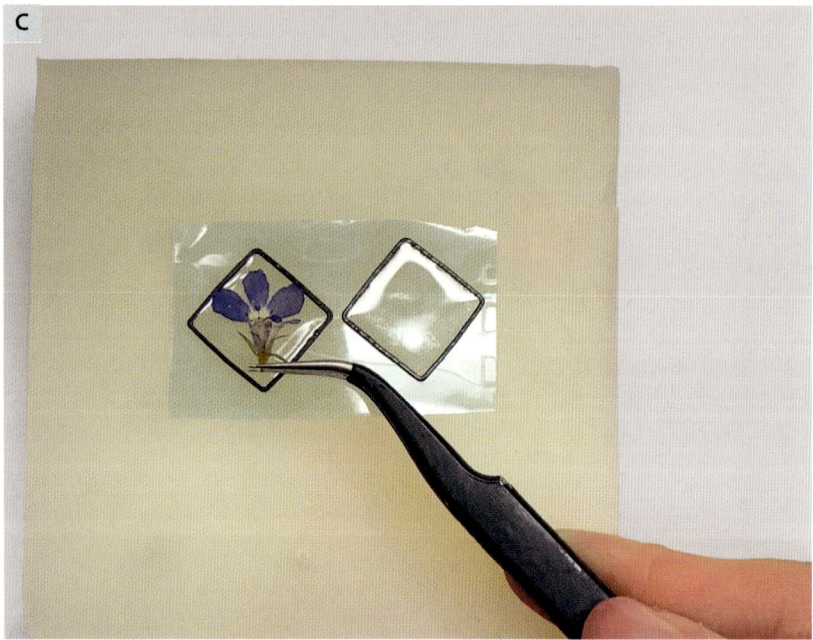

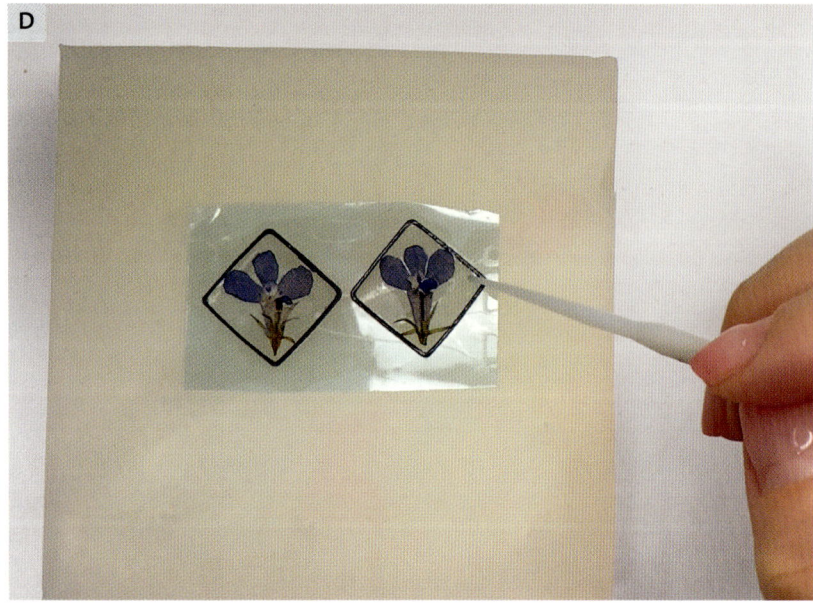

1. Clean the bezels thoroughly with an alcohol wipe.

2. Cut a piece of resin tape and place it sticky side up on a silicone block. Place the larger square pendant bezels onto the tape. Press them down using a soft-gripped pen to secure a tight seal (**A**).

3. Squeeze UV resin into the bezel to form a thin base layer (**B**). Remove all air bubbles using a plastic rod or toothpick.

4. Use tweezers to place a lobelia flower in the center of each bezel (**C**). Cure under a UV lamp for 2 minutes.

5. Apply a second layer of UV resin to form a slight dome over the surface. Remove all air bubbles using a plastic rod or toothpick (**D**). Cure under a UV lamp for another 2 minutes.

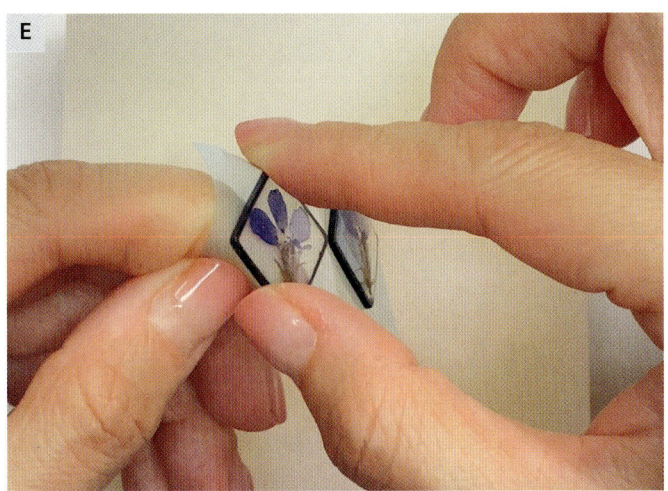

6. Carefully peel the resin tape from the back of the bezel (F).

7. Apply a thin coat of UV resin to the back to mask any tape marks or imperfections (F), then cure under the UV lamp for 2 minutes.

8. Use a handheld jewelry drill to make two small holes near the top and bottom center of each pendant, approximately 2mm from the edge (G). This is where the jump rings will be attached. Use a powder brush to remove any dust or debris from the drilling.

9. Insert a jump ring through the top hole and the earring stud for each earring.

10. Insert a jump ring through each bottom hole and add a tassel to finish (H).

Project 19:
Oval fall leaf earrings

Collecting fallen leaves in autumn is always a delight – the variety of colors and shades feels like nature's own artwork. For these earrings, ordinary fall leaves are carefully trimmed to fit oval frames, creating button-like earrings that showcase the leaves' natural beauty. The design captures the warm, earthy essence of fall, making it a perfect accessory to complement neutral or warm-toned outfits, bringing a touch of seasonal charm to your look.

You will need

- Two oval open bezels (1 x ⅝in (25 x 15mm))
- Alcohol wipe
- Silica-dried oak leaves
- Silicone block
- Black ink pen
- Scissors
- Resin tape
- Soft-gripped pen
- UV resin
- Plastic rod or toothpick
- Tweezers
- UV lamp
- Jewelry pliers (flat nose)
- Thick Cuban chain earrings
- Jewelry findings (two 0.7 x 5mm jump rings in gold-plated stainless steel)

1. Clean the bezels thoroughly with an alcohol wipe.

2. Position an oak leaf on a silicone block. Place the oval bezel over an area of the leaf that you like. Trace around the inside of the bezel using a black pen (**A**), then reposition and repeat.

3. Use scissors to carefully cut out two oval-shaped pieces from the leaf (**B**).

4. Cut a piece of resin tape and place it sticky side up on a silicone block. Press a pendant bezel onto the tape. Use a soft-tipped pen to gently press and rub the bezel to ensure full contact and seal the bottom.

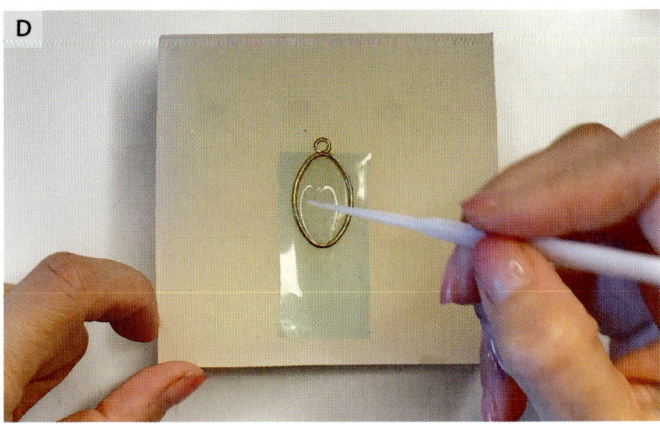

5. Slowly squeeze UV resin into the bezel (**C**), forming a thin, even layer. Use a plastic rod or toothpick to remove any air bubbles (**D**).

115

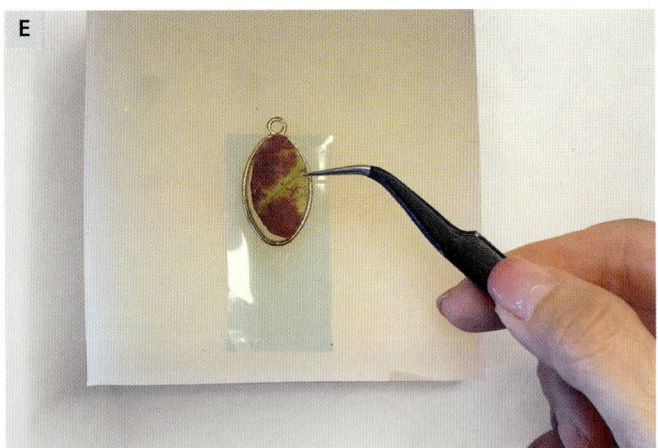

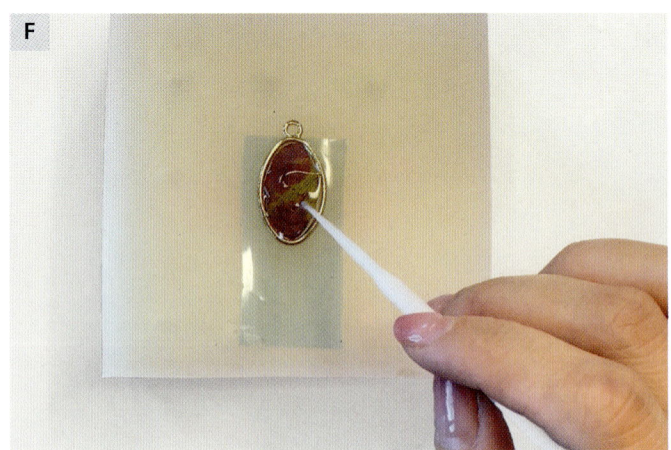

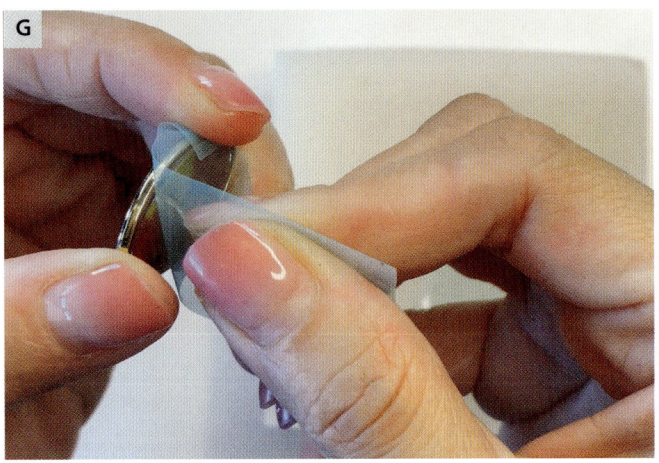

6. Use tweezers to carefully place the oak leaf cutout inside the bezel (E). Cure under a UV lamp for 2 minutes.

7. Apply another layer of UV resin to fully fill the bezel from the front, removing air bubbles with a plastic rod or toothpick (F), and cure for 2 minutes.

8. Carefully peel the resin tape from the back of the bezel (G). Flip it over and apply a thin finishing layer of resin to the back, then cure again for 2 minutes.

9. Use jewelry pliers to insert a jump ring through the bezel's loop and connect it to the end of a Cuban chain earring. Close the jump ring securely. Repeat the process to create the second earring (H).

Project 19 variation:

Round fall leaf earrings

This design is a variation of the oval fall leaf earrings, but in a smaller, round shape. The reduced size allows more colorful leaves to be showcased, giving each pair a vibrant, seasonal character. Instead of cutting the leaf to fit inside the bezel, the bezel is placed directly over the leaf, and any excess is carefully trimmed away. The result is a charming, button-like earring stud – simple to create, yet full of natural fall beauty.

You will need

- As per Project 19, with the following changes:
- Two round open bezels (⅝in (15mm) in diameter) instead of two oval open bezels
- Handheld UV pen
- Jewelry findings (two 6mm flat pad earring posts in gold-plated stainless steel instead of two 0.7 x 5mm jump rings)

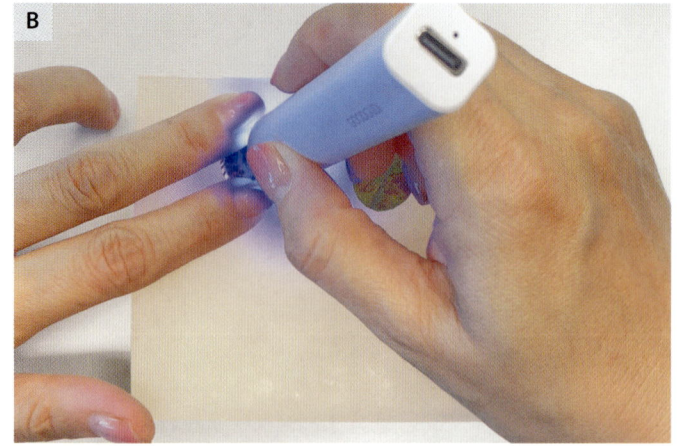

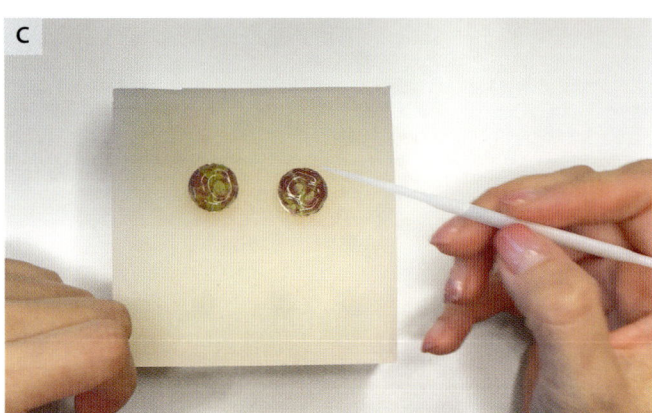

1. Follow Steps 1–3 of the oval fall leaf earrings, this time using the two round open bezels and tracing the outer rather than the inner rims.

2. Apply a thin layer of UV resin to the rims of each bezel. Use tweezers to place the bezels onto the round oak leaf cutouts and gently press down. Cure with a handheld UV pen for 1 minute (B). Trim any excess leaf around the edges of the bezel using scissors.

3. Flip the bezel over, apply UV resin into the recessed areas from the back (C), and cure for 2 minutes.

4. Add another layer of UV resin to the back of the bezel to fully fill the cavity (D) and cure again for 2 minutes. Flip it over and apply a final dome layer to the front surface, then cure for 2 minutes to set.

5. Clean the flat pad of each earring post with alcohol or mild soap. Add a small drop of UV resin to the center back of each bezel and press the posts in place (E). Cure under UV light for 2 minutes.

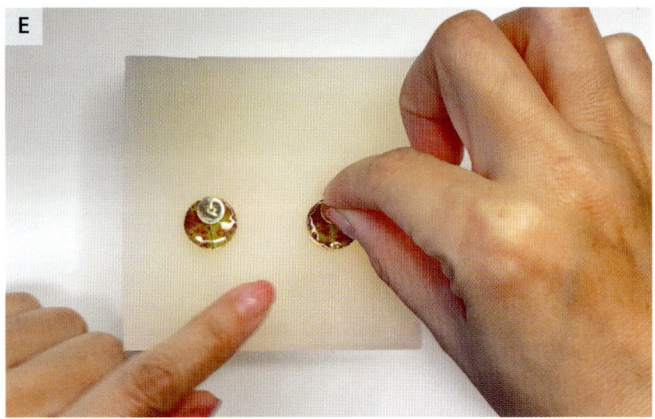

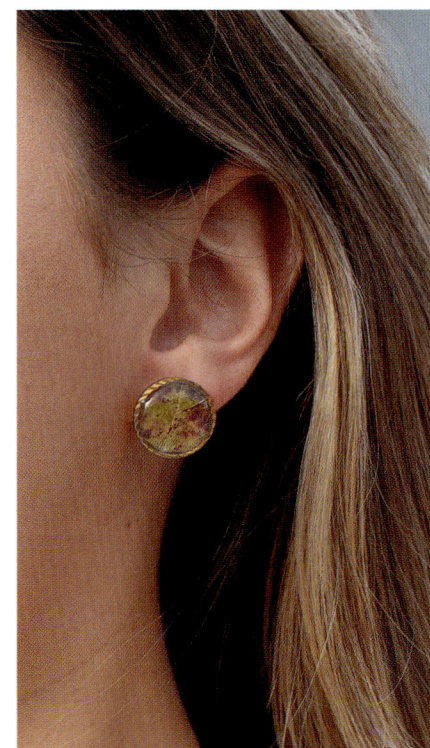

Project 20:

Rabbit ear grass earrings

I n jewelry design, connecting the same element in different sizes often creates a sense of balance and harmony. This piece follows that principle by featuring three bezels, each encapsulating a rabbit ear grass plume of varying size. The arrangement brings a natural flow and a soft, dangling movement, highlighting the delicate texture of the grass while creating a graceful, airy feel.

You will need

- ❀ Six round open bezels (two 1³⁄₈in (35mm), two 1¼in (30mm), two ⁵⁄₈in (15mm) in diameter)
- ❀ Alcohol wipe
- ❀ Resin tape
- ❀ Silicone block
- ❀ Soft-gripped pen
- ❀ UV resin
- ❀ Plastic rod or toothpick
- ❀ Six pressed rabbit ear grass leaves
- ❀ Tweezers
- ❀ UV lamp
- ❀ Handheld drill
- ❀ Stiff foam block or cushion for drilling
- ❀ Powder brush
- ❀ Jewelry pliers (flat nose)
- ❀ Jewelry findings (two ear hooks, six 0.7 x 6mm jump rings all in sterling silver)

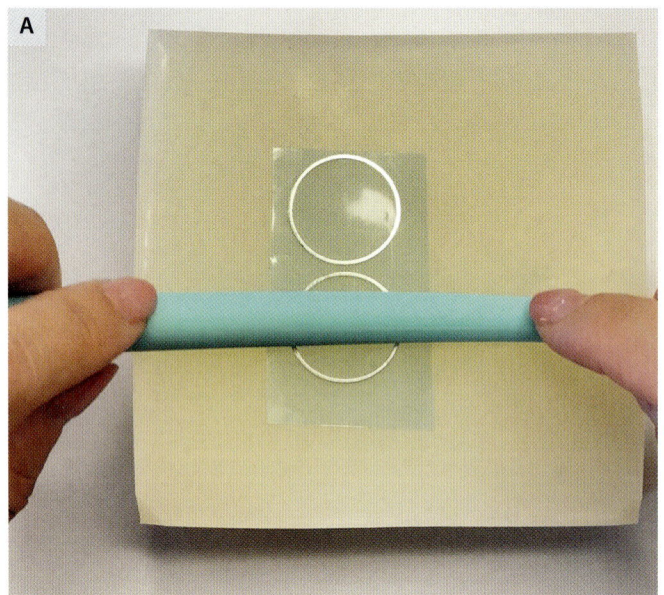

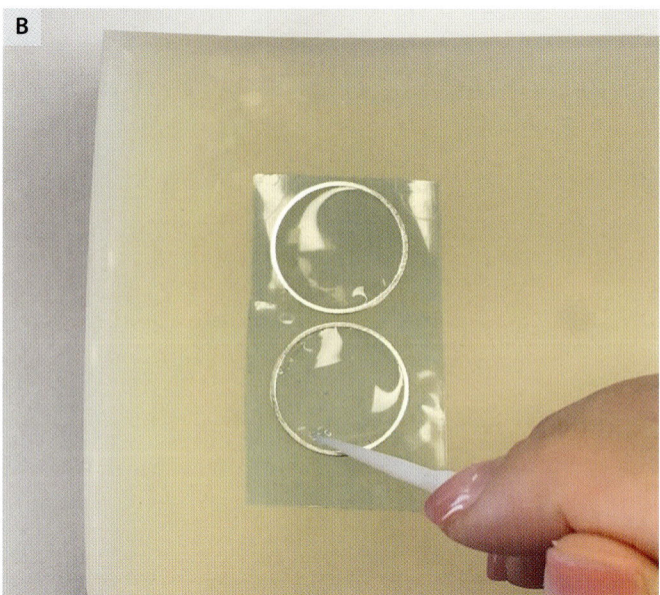

1. Clean the bezels thoroughly with an alcohol wipe.

2. Cut a piece of resin tape and place it sticky side up on a silicone block. Place two pendant bezels onto the tape and press it down using a soft-gripped pen to secure a tight seal (A).

3. Squeeze UV resin into the bezels to form a thin base layer. Remove all air bubbles using a plastic rod or toothpick (B).

4. Use tweezers to place a plume of rabbit ear grass leaves in the center of each bezel and cure for 2 minutes.

5. Apply a second layer of UV resin to form a slight dome over the surface. Remove all air bubbles using a plastic rod or toothpick (C). Cure under a UV lamp for another 2 minutes.

6. Carefully peel the resin tape from the back of each bezel (D).

7. Apply a thin coat of UV resin to the back to mask any tape marks or imperfections, then cure under UV light for 2 minutes.

8. Place on a stiff foam block or cushion and use a handheld jewelry drill to drill two small holes near the top and bottom center of the pendant, approximately 2mm from the edge (E). This is where the jump rings will be attached. Use a powder brush to remove any dust from the drilling.

9. Repeat Steps 2–7 twice more with the medium and small bezels and rabbit grass leaves (F).

10. The assembly of the earrings is done with three jump rings: the first attaches the largest bezel to the ear hook, the second connects the largest bezel to the medium bezel, and the third links the medium bezel to the smallest bezel (G).

Forget-me-not necklace

This necklace features a cluster of side-pressed forget-me-not flowers with delicate sepals, creating a natural and organic composition. The vibrant blue petals, medium-toned green accents and silver foil shavings complement one another beautifully. At 1½in (40mm) in size, the pendant is large enough to make a statement, yet subtle enough to blend effortlessly with any outfit, adding elegance without being overly dramatic.

You will need

- Round open pendant bezel in stainless steel (1½in (40mm) in diameter)
- Alcohol wipe
- Resin tape
- Silicone block
- Soft-gripped pen
- UV resin
- Plastic rod or toothpick
- Pressed whole branch forget-me-not flowers
- Tweezers
- Silver foil shavings
- UV lamp
- Handheld UV pen
- Jewelry pliers (flat nose)
- Jewelry findings (one glue-on bail, one 16–18in (41–46cm) adjustable cable chain necklace both in sterling silver)

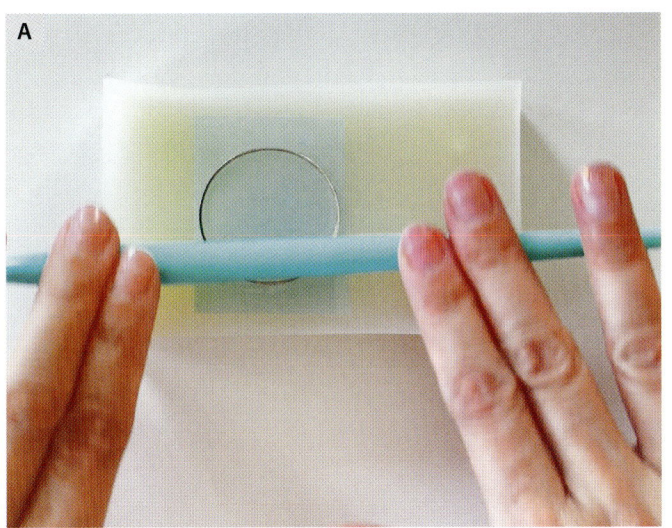

1. Clean the bezel thoroughly with an alcohol wipe.

2. Cut a piece of resin tape and place it sticky side up on a silicone block. Place the pendant bezel onto the tape and press it down using a soft-gripped pen to secure a tight seal (A).

3. Squeeze UV resin into the bezel to form a thin base layer (B). Remove all air bubbles using a plastic rod or toothpick.

4. Use tweezers to position branches of forget-me-not flowers and leaves any way you like (C).

5. Add silver foil shavings to finish the design (D). Cure under UV lamp for 2 minutes.

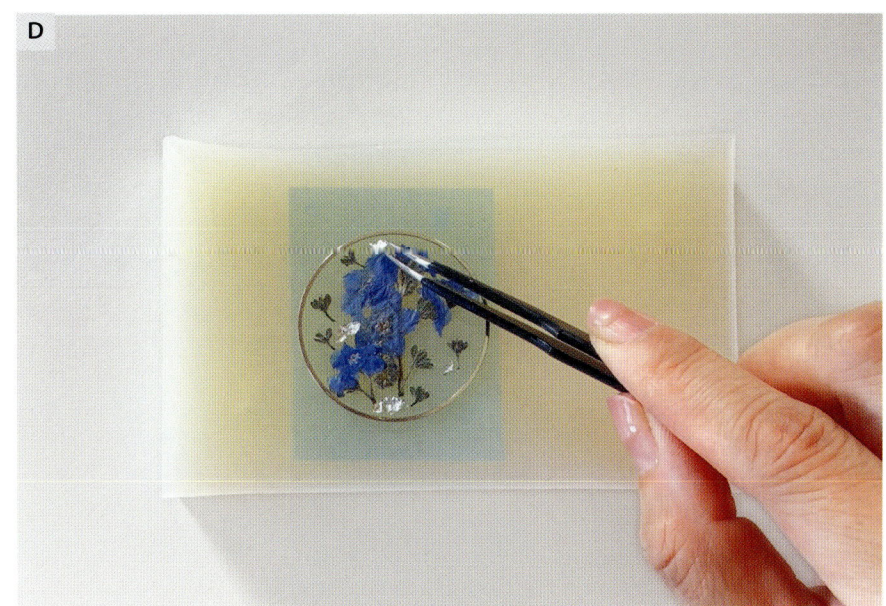

6. Apply a second layer of UV resin on top of the first, slightly overfilling to create a gentle dome effect. Remove all air bubbles using a plastic rod or toothpick (E), then cure under a UV lamp for 2 minutes.

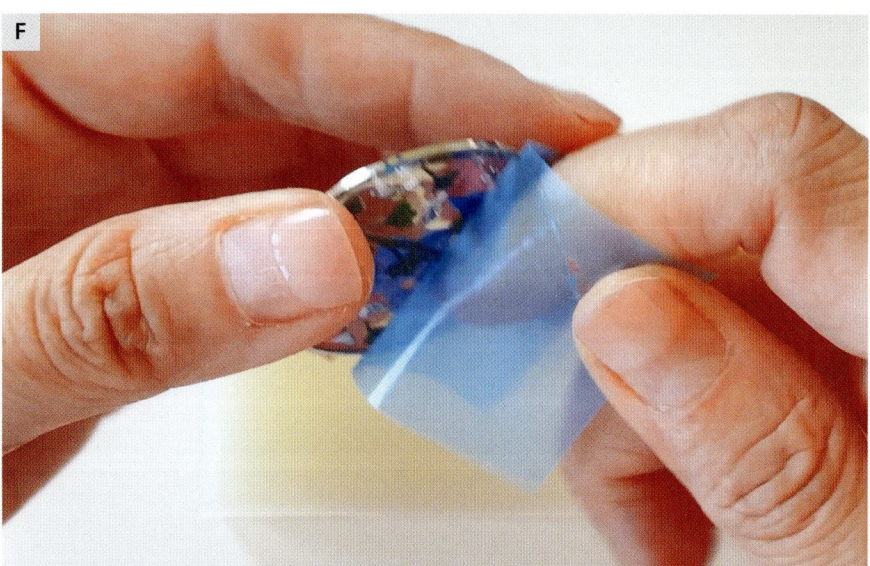

7. Once cured, slowly peel the resin tape from the back of the piece (F).

8. Apply a thin layer of UV resin to cover any tape marks or imperfections (G), then cure under UV light for another 2 minutes.

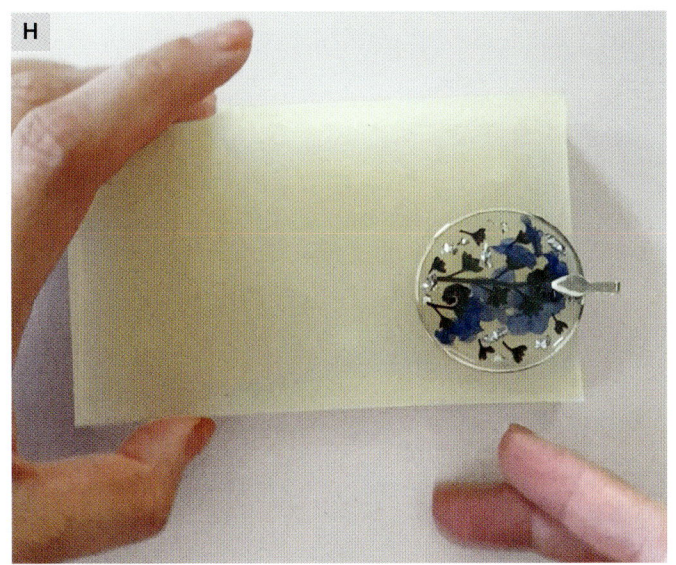

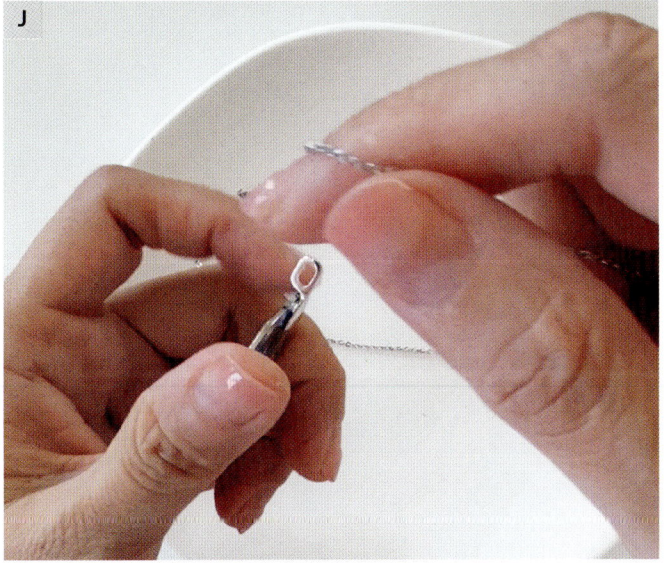

9. Glue a bail to the back using a small drop of UV resin (**H**).

10. Cure under a handheld UV pen to secure the bail (**I**).

11. Once set, insert the necklace chain through the bail to finish (**J**).

Project 22:

Purple verbena earrings

Verbena is a popular flower in home gardens, admired not only for its wide range of colors but also for being an excellent pollinator plant that attracts butterflies and bees. In this design, the verbena's light purple-blue petals with alternating white stripes create a striking and delicate look. To highlight this natural beauty, butterfly-themed decorative charms were added to the earrings, echoing the way real butterflies are drawn to the blooms.

You will need

- ❀ Waterdrop-shaped open bezel in stainless steel
- ❀ Alcohol wipe
- ❀ Resin tape
- ❀ Silicone block
- ❀ Soft-gripped pen
- ❀ UV resin
- ❀ Plastic rod or toothpick
- ❀ Tweezers
- ❀ Pressed purple verbena flowers
- ❀ UV lamp
- ❀ Jewelry pliers (flat nose)
- ❀ Jewelry findings (two earring hooks, two 0.7 x 6mm jump rings all in gold-plated stainless steel)
- ❀ Two butterfly charms in gold-plated stainless steel

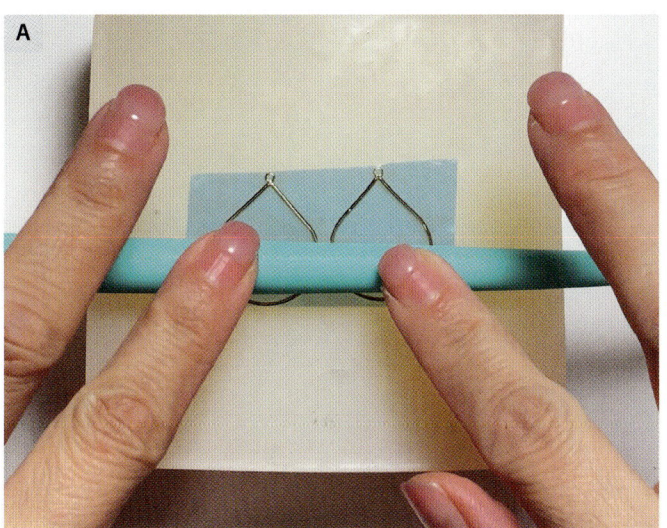

1. Clean the bezel thoroughly with an alcohol wipe.

2. Cut a piece of resin tape and place it sticky side up on a silicone block. Place the pendant bezels onto the tape and press them down with a soft-gripped pen to secure a tight seal (**A**).

3. Squeeze UV resin into the bezel to form a thin base layer (**B**). Remove all air bubbles using a plastic rod or toothpick.

4. Use tweezers to place the purple verbena flowers face up (**C**). Cure under UV lamp for 2 minutes.

5. Apply a second layer of UV resin over the first, slightly overfilling to create a gentle dome. Remove any air bubbles with a plastic rod or toothpick (**D**) and cure for 2 minutes.

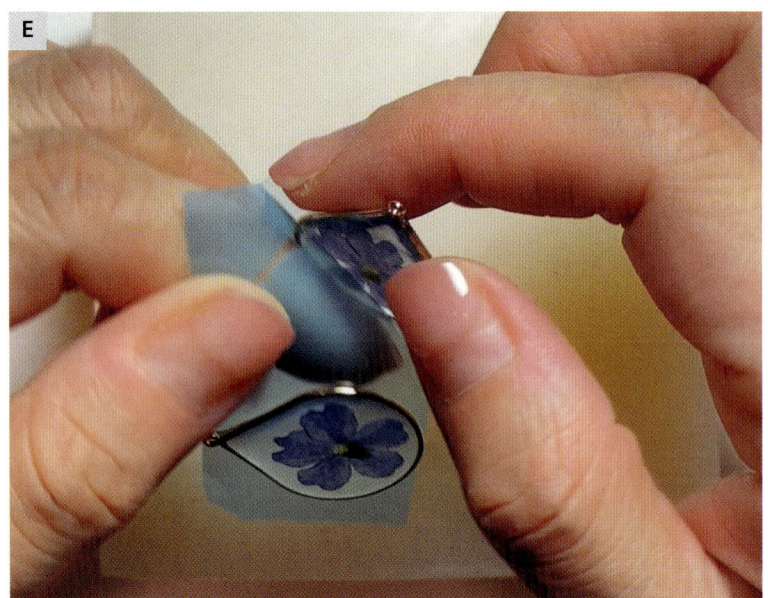

E

6. Once cured, slowly peel the resin tape from the back of the piece (**E**).

7. Apply a thin coat of UV resin to the back to cover any tape marks or imperfections, then cure under UV light for 2 minutes.

8. Take one jump ring and thread it through the top loop of the verbena pendant.

9. Slide the ear hook onto the same jump ring. Add the butterfly charm to the same jump ring (**F**). Close the jump ring securely to connect all three components together. Repeat Steps 8 and 9 with the second earring (**G**).

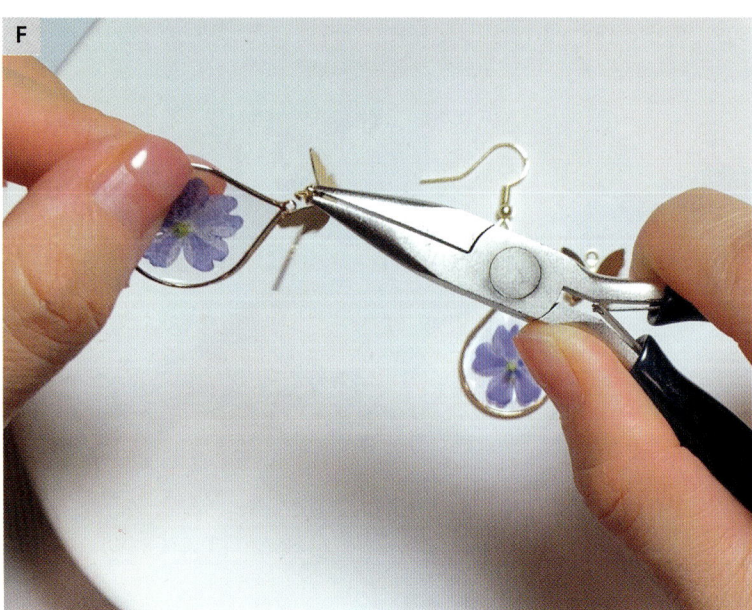

F

G

Project 23:

Rose petal necklace

This design uses pressed petals from miniature roses. The petals are naturally heart-shaped, making them perfect for jewelry. You can enhance their beauty by adding gold gravel or fine metal shavings, which bring a warm and elegant tone to the piece. For the setting, a round bezel works beautifully, as shown in this design, but diamond-shaped or square bezels are also excellent choices to complement the petals' natural charm.

You will need

- Round open bezel (1in (25mm) in diameter)
- Alcohol wipe
- Resin tape
- Silicone block
- Soft-gripped pen
- UV resin
- Plastic rod or toothpick
- Tweezers
- Pressed miniature rose
- Gold gravel
- UV lamp
- Jewelry pliers (flat nose)
- Jewelry findings (ready-made 40-15mm adjustable cable chain in gold-plated stainless steel)

1. Clean the bezel thoroughly with an alcohol wipe.

2. Cut a piece of resin tape and place it sticky side up on a silicone block. Place the pendant bezel onto the tape and press it down with a soft-gripped pen to secure a tight seal (A).

3. Squeeze UV resin into the bezel to form a thin base layer (B). Remove all air bubbles using a plastic rod or toothpick.

4. Use tweezers to add two rose petals in the center of the bezel, arranging them as you like (C).

5. Add gold gravel to fill the spaces (D). Cure under a UV lamp for 2 minutes.

6. Apply a second layer of UV resin over the first, slightly overfilling to create a gentle dome (E), and cure under a UV lamp for 2 minutes.

7. Once cured, slowly peel the resin tape from the back of the piece (F).

8. Apply a thin coat of UV resin to the back to cover any tape marks or imperfections. Remove any bubbles with a plastic rod or toothpick (G), then cure under a UV lamp for 2 minutes.

9. Use jewelry pliers to insert a jump ring through the loop attached to the bezel to connect the chain to the pendant (H).

Working with Molds

This chapter takes your flower resin jewelry craft to the next level by introducing the use of silicone molds. If Chapters 4 and 5 helped you build confidence in encapsulation and working with bezels, this chapter opens up a world of sculptural creativity. Here, your projects will grow in depth – both literally and figuratively – as you cast, layer, and assemble unique resin pieces using a wide range of molds.

Projects in this chapter range from medium to difficult. The simpler ones involve single-pour casting, while the more advanced projects guide you through layer-by-layer resin work, multi-mold designs, and complex jewelry assembly.

Creating your own silicone molds

Silicone molds offer incredible versatility. You can purchase a variety of jewelry molds from craft stores like Etsy, or you can make your own custom molds at home using natural materials – acorns, leaves, seashells, and more.

Here is a step-by-step tutorial on how to create your own silicone molds from acorns, giving your jewelry a completely personalized and organic touch.

Creating your own acorn silicone molds

You will need

- ✿ Clean, dry acorns or other natural items (e.g., shell, nut, flower bud)
- ✿ Small container (to hold the mold, e.g., paper cup, paper or plastic box)
- ✿ Hot glue or double-sided tape
- ✿ Silicone mold-making resin kit (two components: Part A – silicone base, Part B – curing agent)
- ✿ Measuring scale
- ✿ Gloves
- ✿ Mixing cups
- ✿ Stir sticks

1. Choose clean, dry acorns with no cracks. Remove the caps. Use a small container slightly larger than the acorns. Position each acorn with the pointed tip facing upward and the cap end glued to the bottom of the container using small dots of hot glue or double-sided tape to keep them from floating (A).

2. Follow the instructions on your silicone kit (most are 1:1 ratio by volume). Wearing gloves, pour equal volumes of parts A and B into a mixing cup. Use stir sticks to mix slowly and thoroughly for 2–3 minutes, scraping the sides and bottom (B).

3. Slowly pour the mixed silicone resin into the container, starting at one corner to reduce bubbles. Completely cover the acorns with at least $^3/_8$ in (1cm) of silicone above the highest point (C).

4. Allow the mold to sit undisturbed for the time recommended on your product label, usually 6–12 hours (D). To prevent dust from settling, cover the mold lightly with a clean, flat object such as a cut-down clear box lid.

5. Once fully cured, gently peel away the container. Remove the acorns from the mold by pulling, cutting, or slicing carefully, if needed (E).

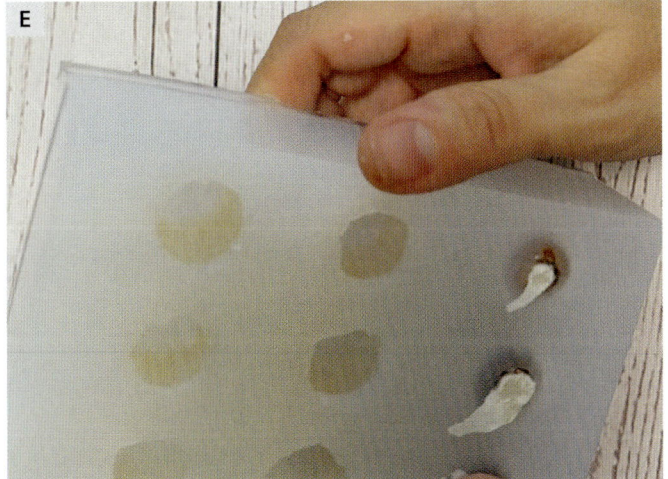

How to care for silicone molds

Before diving into the projects, it's important to understand how to care for and clean your silicone molds properly because well-maintained molds are key to getting clear, bubble-free, and beautifully shaped resin pieces. Store molds flat in a cool, dry place, out of direct sunlight, and avoid stacking them with sharp or heavy objects to prevent deformation.

Cleaning the molds

Before starting any project, it's essential to clean your silicone mold thoroughly.

Take a small piece of clear packing tape and gently press it against the inside walls and base of the mold. Peel it away to lift off dust, debris, and tiny fibers without scratching or damaging the surface. Repeat with fresh tape as needed. For a mold for an item such as an acorn, which is deep with a small aperture, use your finger or a cotton swab to press down the tape as far as you can.

Avoid rinsing the mold with water right before use as residual moisture can lead to cloudiness or air bubbles in the resin. Do not use harsh chemicals or alcohol to clean molds, as they may cause surface damage or dullness.

Designing with molds

When designing with molds, remember that the bottom of the mold often becomes the front-facing surface of your finished piece. The widest part of the item should usually be the entry point. This allows the resin to flow easily into all the detailed parts during casting and makes demolding easier, without damaging the mold or the cast object. A flat base creates a clean mold opening; however, the mold can be trimmed later too. Trimming makes the object flat, so it sits securely.

Use only soft tools like plastic or silicone sticks when working inside the mold; metal tools can scratch and damage the mold surface.

Unlike bezel settings, mold-based designs require careful layering. Lightweight materials like flower petals tend to float to the top, while heavier elements like gravel may sink. Plan your designs accordingly, building them layer by layer to achieve the desired final look.

Project 24:

Blue cornflower earrings

This dainty design is perfect for beginners working with molds. The earrings feature pressed blue cornflower petals in a charming waterdrop shape, creating a simple yet elegant silhouette. A pearl is added to guide the eye and enhance the overall flow, giving the piece a graceful and refined appearance.

You will need

- UV resin
- Silicone mold with small teardrop shape
- Silicone block
- Plastic rod or toothpick
- Tweezers
- Gold gravel
- Silica-dried blue cornflower flower petals
- UV lamp
- Handheld UV pen

- Handheld drill
- Stiff foam block or cushion for drilling
- Powder brush
- Jewelry pliers (flat nose)
- Jewelry findings (two 0.7 x 5mm jump rings, two ear hooks all in gold-plated stainless steel)
- 4mm pearl bead connector with eye pins on both ends

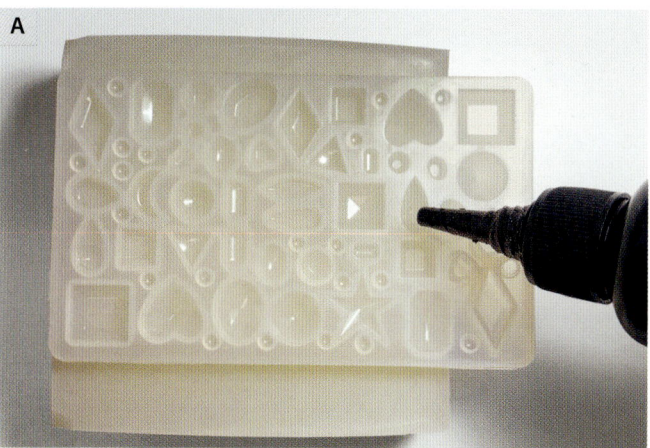

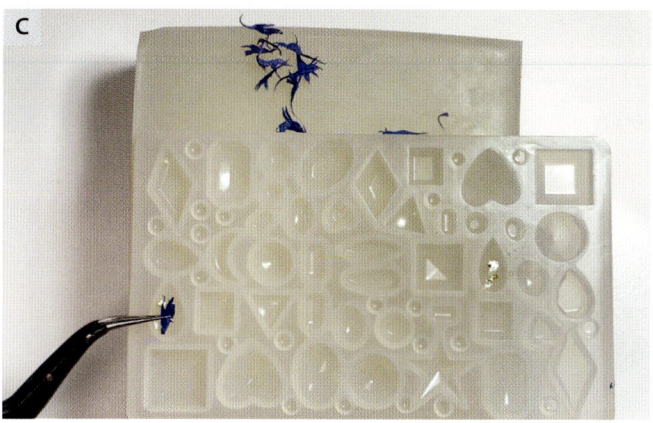

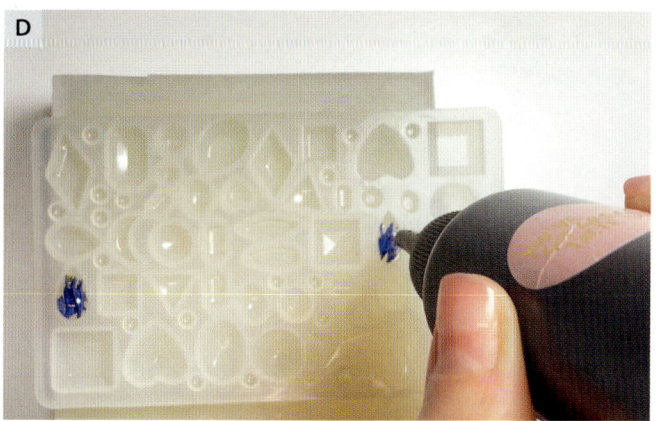

1. Gently squeeze in enough UV resin to fill about one-third of the mold placed on a silicone block (A). Let it settle evenly across the base and remove air bubbles with a plastic rod or toothpick.

2. Using tweezers or a plastic rod, place a few pieces of gold gravel into the resin (B).

3. Add two or three blue cornflower petals and arrange them to your liking (C).

4. If desired, add a few more pieces of gold gravel to the surface and gently reposition them with a stick to enhance the design. Make sure everything is secure and visually balanced.

5. Add another drop of resin to seal the petals, remove any air bubbles with a plastic rod or toothpick (D), and cure under UV lamp for 2 minutes.

6. Add more UV resin to fill the mold to the top. Let the resin spread evenly and cure again under UV light for another 2 minutes.

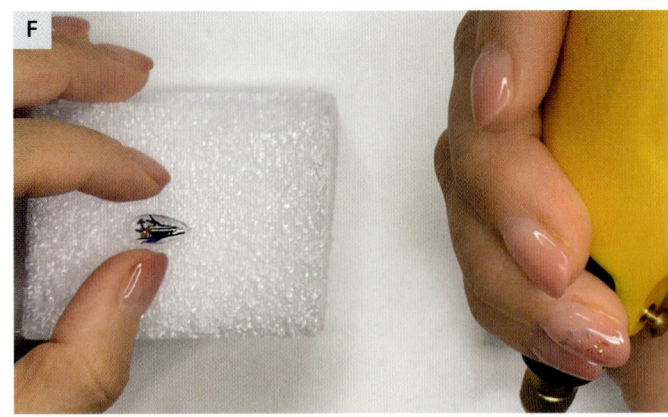

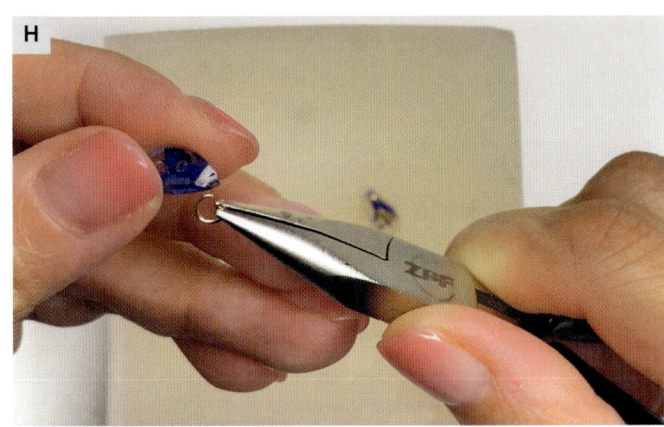

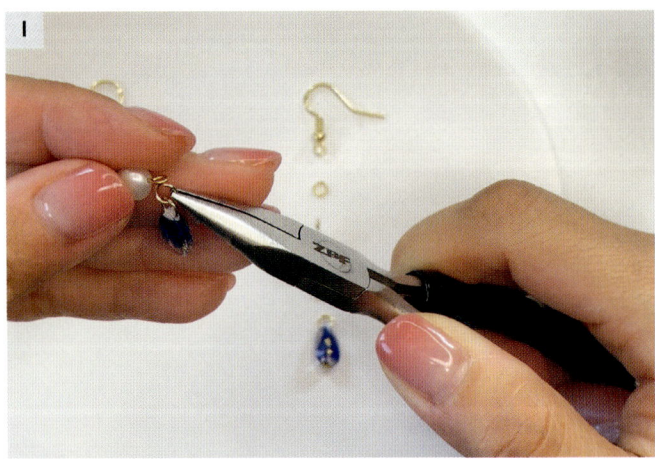

7. Once set, carefully pop the resin pieces out of the mold (E).

8. After the resin is fully cured and hardened, place onto a stiff foam block or cushion and use a handheld jewelry drill to make a small hole near the top, about 2mm from the edge (F). This is where your jump ring will go.

9. Dust off the loose dust from the drilling with a powder brush (G).

10. Use jewelry pliers to insert a jump ring through each hole (H).

11. Attach the pearl connector (I).

12. Attach another jump ring and an ear hook to the jump ring (J). Repeat the process to create the second earring.

Project 25:

Acorn necklace

This necklace features a charming acorn-shaped pendant, created using a mold made from real acorns (see p.134). Inside the pendant, you can encapsulate delicate flowers, botanical components, or even tiny crystals, transforming it into a miniature crystal ball. The design combines natural inspiration with creative flexibility, making it an earthy and versatile accessory.

You will need

- Two-component epoxy resin
- Measuring scales
- Small paper mixing cup
- Gloves
- Plastic rod or toothpick
- Vacuum chamber (optional)
- Silicone mold with acorn shape (see p.134)
- Matte UV nail polish topcoat
- Air-dried purple statice flowers, silica-dried rose buds, and other flowers
- Tweezers
- Handheld UV pen
- Jewelry pliers (flat nose and cutting pliers)
- Nail stand
- Caps from natural acorns
- Small handheld drill
- Stiff foam block or cushion for drilling
- Powder brush
- Jewelry findings (two screw eye pins, one 0.7 x 6mm jump ring all in bronze)
- 18in (46 cm) cord necklace in dark brown

1. Begin by preparing the epoxy resin. Measure the resin and hardener according to the ratio indicated on the label, using measuring scales and a small paper cup (**A**).

2. Wearing gloves, stir the two components together thoroughly for 2 minutes with a plastic rod or toothpick (**B**), making sure to scrape the sides and bottom of the cup to ensure a uniform mix.

3. To remove air bubbles, place the mixture in a vacuum chamber for 5 minutes (**C**). If a vacuum chamber isn't available, you can let the cup sit in warm water to help the bubbles rise and pop naturally.

4. Fix the flowers into the mold using UV resin. Start by applying a thin layer of nail polish topcoat into the bottom of the mold to create a base layer.

5. Place the flowers carefully into the resin using tweezers (**D**).

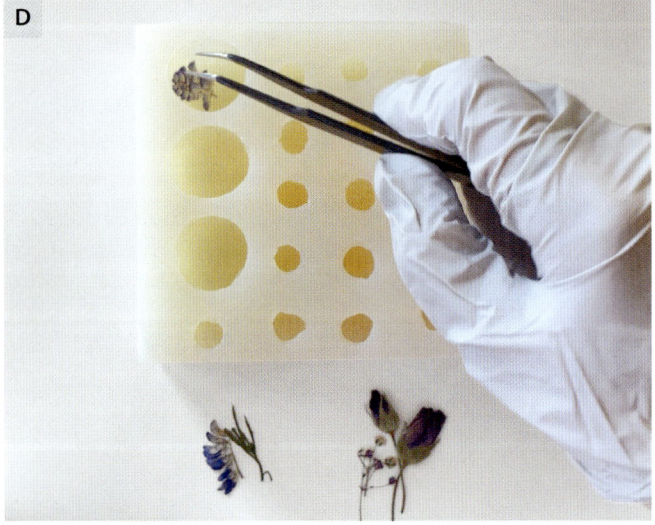

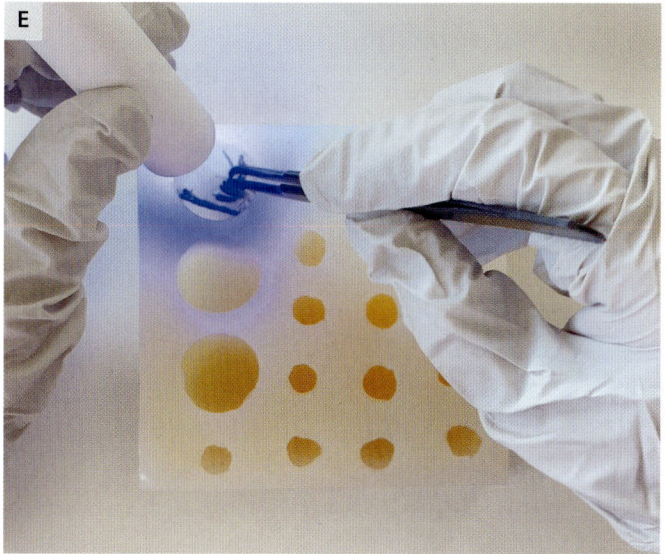

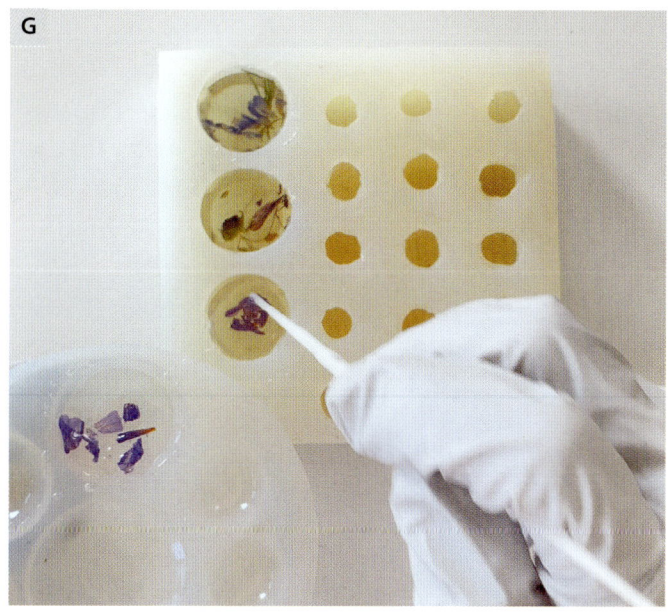

6. Cure the flowers in place using a handheld UV pen for 2 minutes (E). Repeat this process until all desired flowers are positioned and secured.

7. Once the flowers are fixed, slowly pour the epoxy resin into the mold until it's about halfway full (F).

8. Watch for any air bubbles and gently drag them to the edges with a plastic rod or toothpick to help them pop (G).

9. Let the resin sit for about 30 minutes to thicken, which helps hold the flowers in place. At this stage, you can also add flower petals such as

purple statice; some petals may naturally float toward the top, which adds a layered effect.

10. After it settles, fill the rest of the mold with resin. Allow the resin to cure undisturbed for 12–14 hours. While the surface will feel solid to the touch at that point, it will continue to cure over the next 72 hours.

11. Once fully hardened, gently demold the acorn pendant and inspect it (H). If any surface imperfections are visible, apply a thin layer of UV resin and cure it under UV light to smooth and seal the finish.

12. After demolding, use cutting pliers to trim the edges of the acorn pendant for a clean finish (I).

13. Place the pendant on a nail stand and apply a thin coat of UV resin over the surface to enhance its shine (J), then cure under the UV lamp for 2 minutes.

14. Next, prepare the acorn cap. Trim off the stem using cutting pliers (K).

15. Use a few drops of UV resin to glue the cap securely onto the pendant (L). Cure under UV light for 2 minutes.

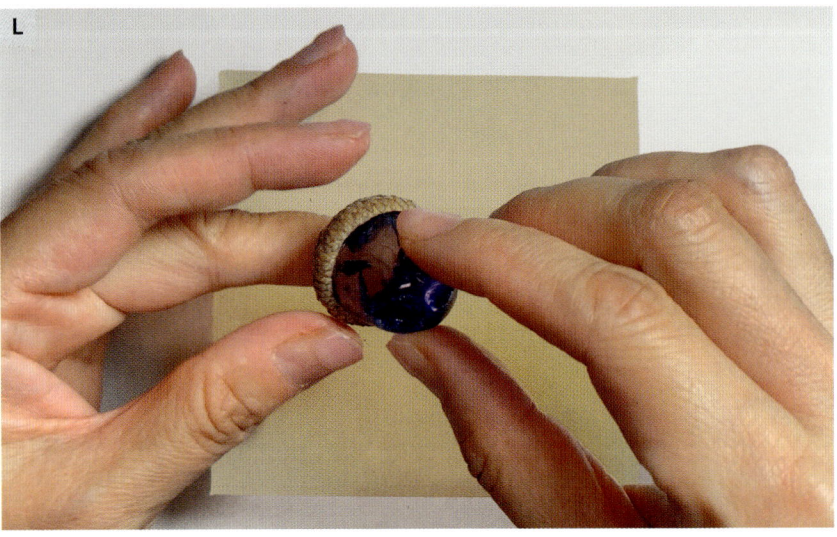

16. To complete the pendant, drill a small hole about 3–4mm deep into the center of the acorn cap (M). Brush off any dust from drilling using a powder brush.

17. Apply a small amount of UV resin to the tip of an eye pin and screw it into the hole using jewelry pliers until it is firmly in place (N). For added durability and a clean look, brush a matte UV topcoat around the connection point and cure for 2 minutes.

18. Finally, use jewelry pliers to insert a jump ring through the eye pin and attach it to a leather cord necklace to finish the acorn pendant (O).

Project 26:

Forget-me-not earrings

These earrings feature individually front-pressed forget-me-not flowers, showcasing their delicate light-blue petals. The design is romantic and subtle yet intricate in detail. The mold used is slightly larger than the waterdrop mold from previous projects, making it ideal for practicing the "layer-by-layer" technique when filling molds, allowing for greater control and depth in your resin work.

You will need

- ❀ UV resin
- ❀ Silicone mold with square shape
- ❀ Plastic rod or toothpick
- ❀ Tweezers
- ❀ Pressed forget-me-not flowers
- ❀ UV lamp
- ❀ Silicone block
- ❀ 3mm half pearls
- ❀ Jewelry pliers (flat nose)
- ❀ Jewelry findings (two flat-back ear studs in sterling silver)

1. Gently squeeze in enough UV resin to fill about one-third of the square mold. Let it settle evenly across the base and remove air bubbles with a plastic rod or toothpick (**A**).

2. Using tweezers, carefully place four or five forget-me-not flowers face down, spacing them to cover the surface evenly. Press gently, if needed, to keep them flat. Cure under a UV lamp for 2 minutes.

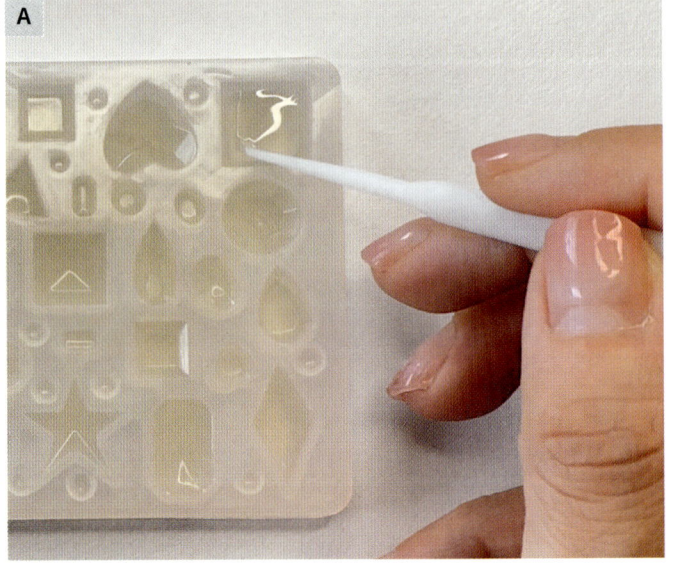

A

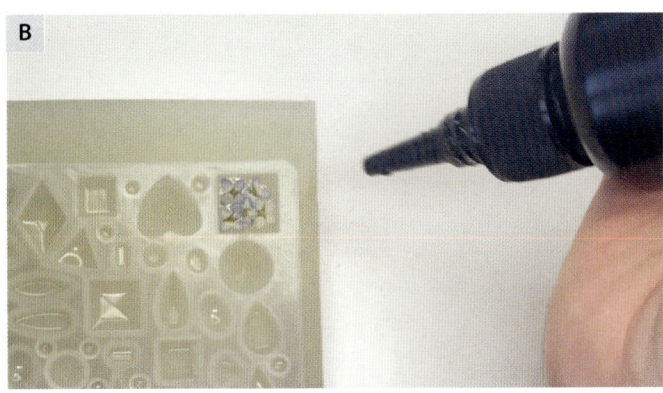

3. Add more UV resin to fill the mold completely (**B**). Cure again for 2 minutes.

4. Gently remove the cured piece from the mold.

5. Place the demolded piece with flower side up on a silicone block. Apply a thin line of UV resin along the lower edges (**C**).

6. Use tweezers to place tiny half pearls along the resin line (**D**). Once you're happy with the layout, cure under UV lamp for 2 minutes.

7. Apply a small drop of UV resin to the back of the pendant (**E**) and attach a stud earring backing using jewelry pliers. Press it gently into place and cure for 2 minutes.

8. Repeat to create the second earring (**F**).

White daisy earrings

This project uses a mold with intricate details, including sharp corners and undercuts. Because the mold is not transparent, UV resin alone is not ideal; instead, a two-component epoxy resin like the one used in the acorn necklace will be used, following the same preparation method. UV resin is then applied to attach the pressed flower to the cured epoxy base, allowing you to continue building the resin flower piece layer by layer. The result is a delicate, detailed white daisy design with a realistic and elegant finish.

You will need

- Two-component epoxy resin
- Measuring scales
- Small paper mixing cup
- Gloves
- Plastic rod or toothpick
- Vacuum chamber (optional)
- Silicone mold with daisy flower shape

- UV resin
- Plastic rod or toothpick
- UV lamp
- Tweezers
- Two pressed white daisy flowers
- Handheld UV pen
- Irregular round open bezel (1⅜in (35mm) in diameter)

- Silicone block
- Nail file
- Jewelry pliers (flat nose)
- Jewelry findings (two 0.7 x 5mm jump rings, two ear hooks all in gold-plated stainless steel)

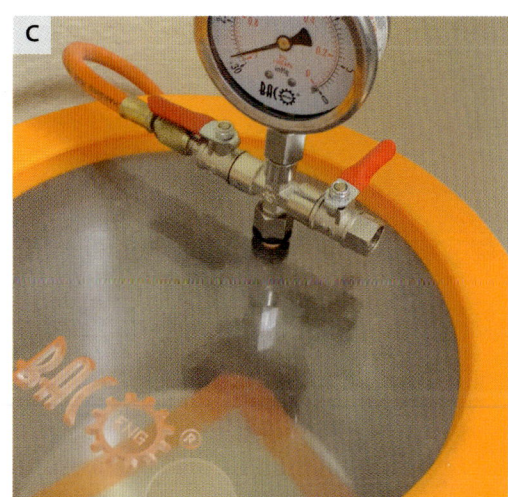

1. Begin by preparing the epoxy resin. Measure the resin and hardener according to the ratio indicated on the label, using measuring scales and a small paper cup (**A**).

2. Wearing gloves, stir the two components together thoroughly for 2 minutes with a plastic rod or toothpick (**B**), making sure to scrape the sides and bottom of the cup to ensure a uniform mix.

3. To remove air bubbles, place the mixture in a vacuum chamber for 5 minutes (**C**). If a vacuum chamber isn't available, you can let the cup sit in warm water to help the bubbles rise and pop naturally.

4. Fill the mold with the epoxy resin. Let it settle evenly and remove any bubbles with a plastic rod or toothpick (**D**).

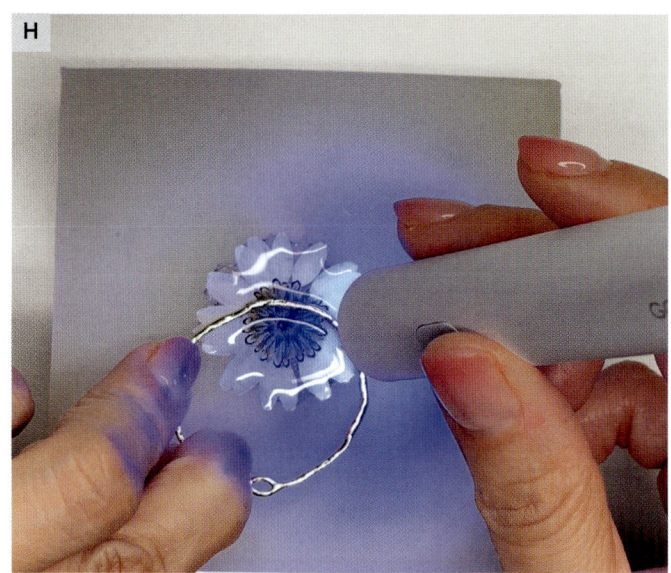

5. Apply a thin coat of UV resin on top and use tweezers to gently press a daisy flower upside down into the resin (**E**). Make sure the flower is fully in contact with the resin to avoid bubbles. Cure under UV light for another 2 minutes.

6. Once cured, carefully demold the piece (**F**).

7. Inspect the front and apply UV resin to fill in any small holes or rough edges caused by bubbles (**G**). Smooth the surface and cure again for 2 minutes.

8. Place the flower pendant flat on a silicone block with the decorative (front) side facing down. Apply UV resin to the underside, then position the round bezel so its edge aligns with the center of the pendant. Cure under a handheld UV pen for 2 minutes to secure everything in place (**H**).

9. Check the edges with your fingers and gently file any sharp spots using a nail file (I).

10. Add a final layer of UV resin over the whole surface for a polished finish (J). Cure for 2 minutes one last time.

11. Use jewelry pliers to insert a jump ring through the hole in the bezel (K).

12. Attach an ear hook and repeat the whole process to make a second daisy pendant earring (L).

Project 28:

Blue and green baby's breath earrings

This project uses two different molds: a larger thin mold for the pendant and a smaller button-like mold for the earring stud. Both are round in shape, and sizes can be varied. You can also choose different flowers and patterns for the two pieces, as long as the colors complement each other. The resin enhances the fluffy texture of the air-dried baby's breath flowers, resulting in youthful, bright, and lively earrings that bring a cheerful and uplifting mood.

You will need

- 🌸 Silicone mold with large ring shape (1½in (40mm))
- 🌸 UV resin
- 🌸 Tweezers
- 🌸 Air-dried blue and green baby's breath flowers
- 🌸 White rice forever flowers
- 🌸 Silver foil shavings
- 🌸 Plastic rod or toothpick
- 🌸 UV lamp
- 🌸 Scissors
- 🌸 Silicone mold with small circular button shape (⅝–¾in (15–20mm) in diameter)
- 🌸 Nail file
- 🌸 Handheld drill
- 🌸 Stiff foam block or any cushion for drilling
- 🌸 Powder brush
- 🌸 Handheld UV pen
- 🌸 Jewelry pliers (flat nose)
- 🌸 Jewelry findings (two 4mm flat pad earrings posts, two 4 x 8mm screwed eye pin, two 0.7 x 5mm jump rings all in sterling silver)

1. To make the pendant, slowly fill about half of the large ring mold with UV resin.

2. Use tweezers to arrange green and blue baby's breath and white rice flowers in an alternating pattern, filling the gaps with silver foil shavings (**A**). Remember, the bottom of the mold will be the front of the pendant. Cure under a UV lamp for 2 minutes.

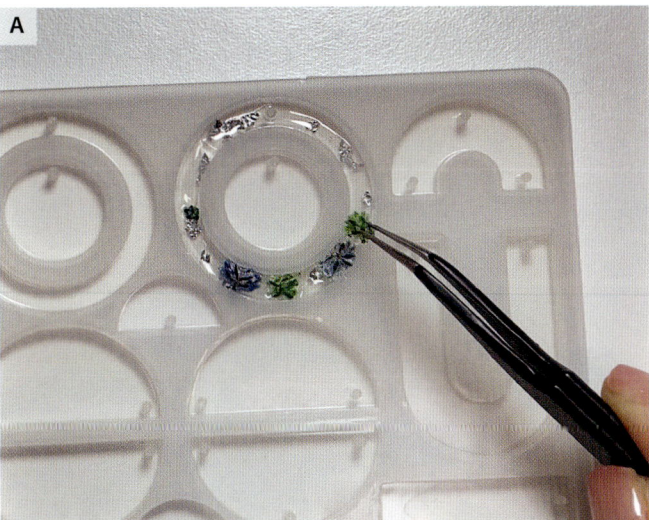

3. Add more resin to fill the mold completely, creating a slight dome (**B**). Use a plastic rod or toothpick to remove any bubbles then cure again under the UV light for 2 minutes.

C

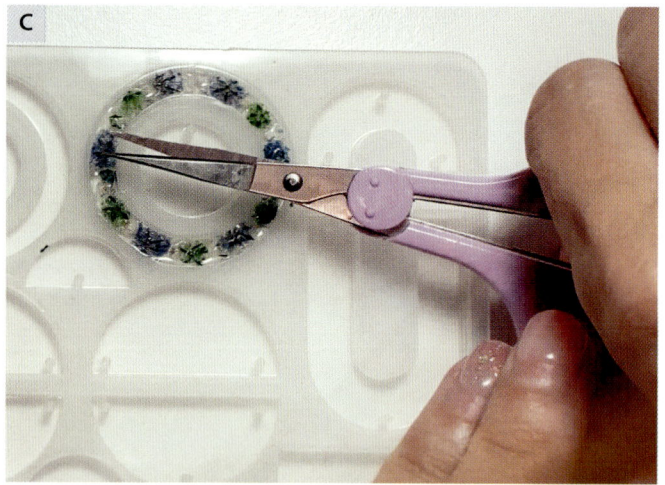

D

E

F

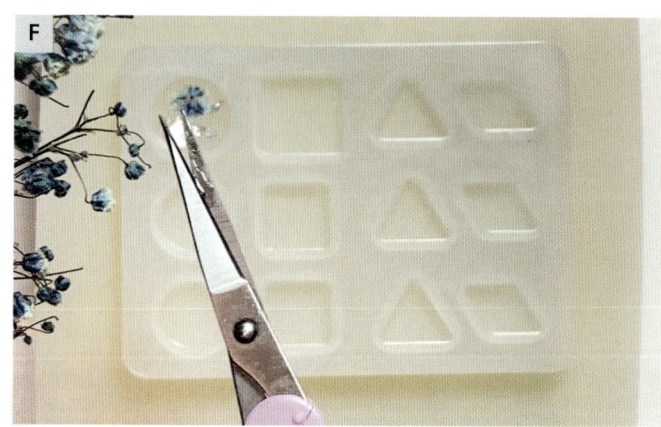

G

4. Air-dried baby's breath flowers are more 3D in nature; use scissors to trim off any flowers that protrude too high from the mold (C).

5. Apply a thin dome layer over the cured surface (D) and cure for 2 minutes once more to finish the pendant.

6. Remove the pendant from the mold.

7. To make the stud, apply a thin layer of UV resin into the button mold (E).

8. Add pieces of green and blue baby's breath, along with silver foil shavings, then cure and trim off any protrusions (F).

9. Slowly top off the mold with more UV resin to form a dome. Remove any bubbles using a plastic rod or toothpick (G), then cure for 2 minutes under UV light.

H

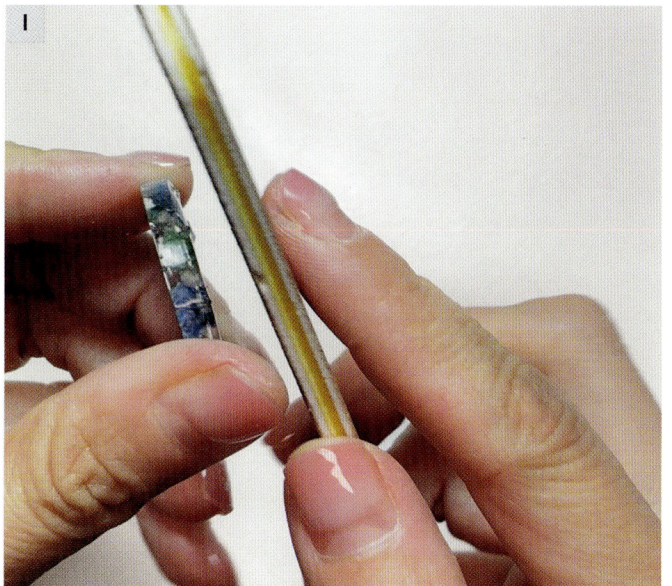

10. Remove the button from the mold (**H**).

11. If the surface of the ring is not smooth due to the texture of the baby's breath flowers, smooth any unevenness using a nail file (**I**) and apply a final coat of resin outside of the mold. Remove any air bubbles with the plastic rod or toothpick.

12. Once both pieces are cured, position the ring pendant upright on foam blocks or a cushion. Drill a 3mm hole near the top using a handheld drill (**J**). Brush off any dust from drilling with a powder brush.

13. Use a plastic rod dipped in UV resin to fill the hole slightly, then insert the screwed eye pin using jewelry pliers (**K**).

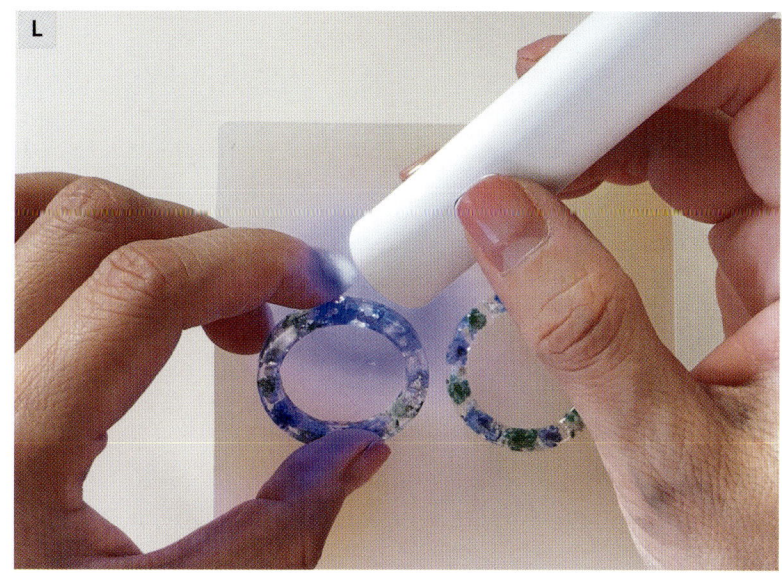

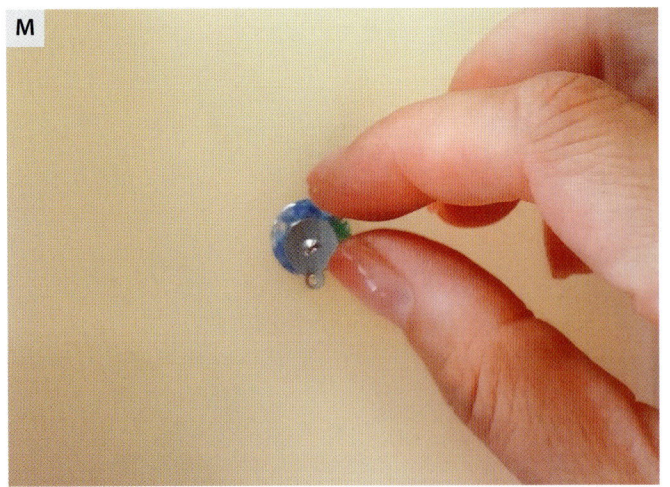

14. Cure with a handheld UV pen for 1 minute (L).

15. Clean the flat pad earring post with alcohol or mild soap to remove any dust or oils. Use a drop of UV resin to attach the post to the center back of the resin stud (M).

16. Cure under a handheld UV pen for 2 minutes (N).

17. Finally, insert a jump ring through the peg on the pendant and through the loop on the stud earring (O).

18. Close the jump ring to connect the pieces into a complete earring. Repeat the process for the second earring (P).

Project 29:

Rice flower earrings

Now that you are familiar with using different molds and the layer-by-layer technique, this project takes it a step further with a larger mold and a more three-dimensional flower layout. Colored resin is incorporated to create a complementary background, enhancing the overall design. This project allows you to explore depth and dimension, resulting in earrings that are vibrant, dynamic, and full of visual interest.

You will need

- Silicone mold with large teardrop shape (1½in (40mm))
- UV resin
- Plastic rod or toothpick
- Tweezers
- Silver gravel
- Gold gravel
- White rice forever flowers
- Air-dried green baby's breath flowers
- UV lamp
- Nail stand
- Silicone mold with hemisphere shape (⅝–¾in (15–20mm) in diameter)
- Silicone mold with hemisphere shape (⅝in (15mm) in diameter)
- White gel nail polish
- Green gel nail polish
- Handheld UV pen
- Nail file
- Jewelry pliers (flat nose)
- Jewelry findings (two 6mm flat pad earrings posts, four 0.7 x 5mm jump rings all in gold-plated stainless steel)

1. Slowly squeeze a small amount of UV resin into two large teardrop molds to about one-third full (**A**). Use a plastic rod or toothpick to remove any bubbles.

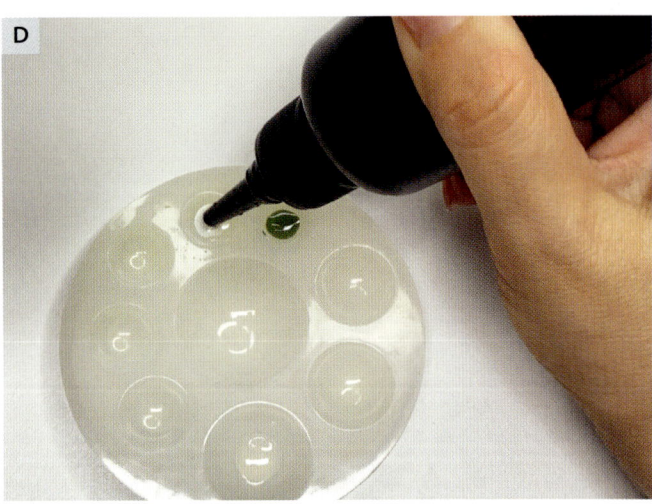

2. Use tweezers to add a few pieces of silver gravel, then place a small cluster of rice flowers and green baby's breath. Cure under a UV lamp for 2 minutes.

3. Apply another layer of UV resin and add a couple of pieces of gold gravel, followed by another small cluster of green baby's breath. Fill the molds completely with UV resin (B).

4. Cure under the UV lamp until fully hardened then remove the pendants from the mold (C).

5. To paint the backs of the pendants, add a few drops of UV resin into a hemisphere mold. Mix in one drop of white nail polish to create colored resin. Repeat the same process to make green UV resin (D).

6. Place the pendants upside down on a nail stand. Use a plastic rod to apply small patches of white

UV resin to the back of each pendant (E) and cure for 2 minutes.

7. Fill the gaps between the white patches with green UV resin to create a mosaic pattern (F), then cure again for 2 minutes.

8. Flip the pendants right side up and place them back on the nail stand.

9. Apply a thin, even layer of UV resin on the front surface and cure with a handheld UV pen for 1 minute (**G**).

10. Smooth any sharp edges using a nail file (**H**).

11. Apply a thin layer of UV resin to the back (**I**).

12. Position a jump ring at the tops of the pendants as bails. Hold them in place and cure the resin around the jump ring with a handheld UV pen (**J**).

13. For the resin studs, fill two-thirds of two stud molds with clear UV resin and cure for 2 minutes. Top them off with the green UV resin and cure again for 2 minutes (**K**). Remove from the mold.

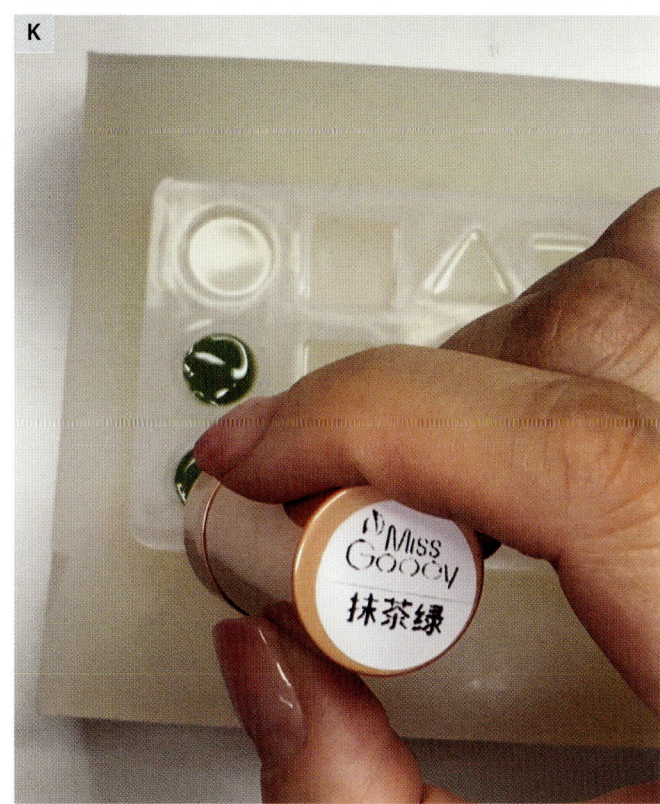

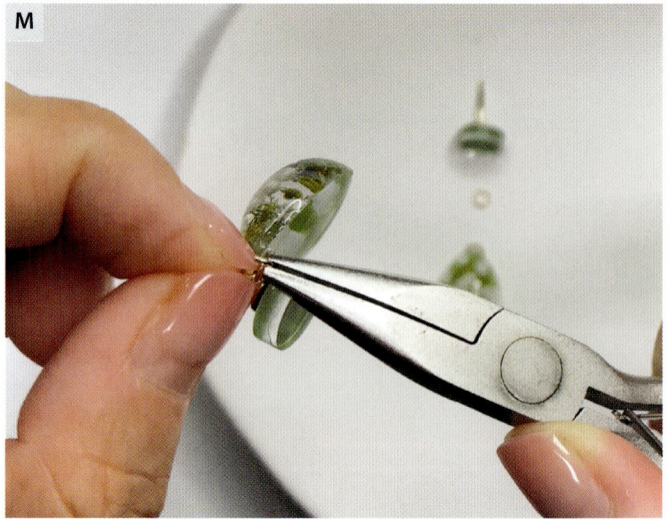

14. Clean the flat pad earring posts with alcohol or mild soap to remove any oils or dust. Use a drop of UV resin to attach a post to the center back of each resin stud (L) and cure under UV light for 2 minutes.

15. Finally, insert a jump ring through the jump ring bail on each pendant (M) and through the loop on each stud earring.

16. Close the jump rings securely to complete the earrings (N).

Project 30:

Purple and white baby's breath pendant

Baby's breath is a delicate flower often found in both natural and dyed shades at local florists. It can be preserved by pressing, which flattens it into a 2D form, or air-drying, which maintains more of its natural 3D structure. For this design, I paired one natural air-dried white bloom with a soft purple-tinted one and set them in a larger teardrop-shaped mold. To create depth, the back was first dusted with blue glitter, then layered with black resin, forming a rich, galaxy-inspired backdrop. The result is a pendant that feels ethereal and timeless, capturing the fragile beauty of flowers against the vastness of the cosmos.

You will need

- Silicone mold with elongated teardrop shape
- UV resin
- Tweezers
- Air-dried baby's breath flowers and buds
- Plastic rod or toothpick
- Silver gravel
- UV lamp
- Blue metal foil shavings
- Black gel nail polish
- Handheld drill

- Stiff foam block or cushion for drilling
- Powder brush
- Jewelry pliers (flat nose)
- Jewelry findings (5mm triangle jump ring, 0.7 x 6mm jump ring both in gold-plated stainless steel)
- Ready-made 16–18in (41–46cm) adjustable necklace in gold-plated stainless steel

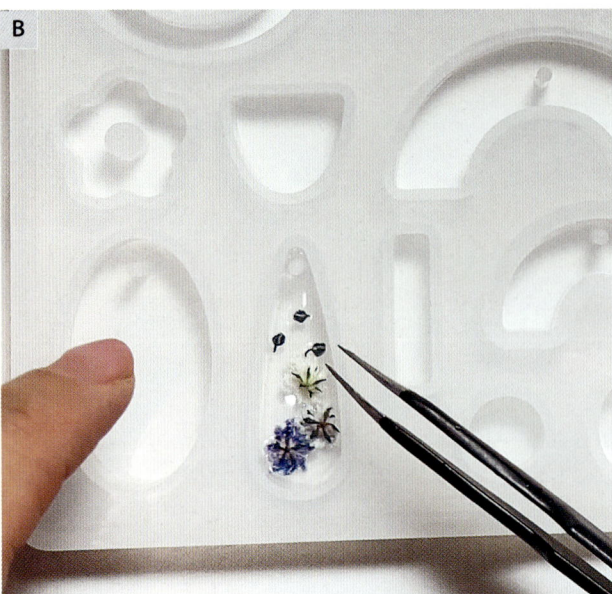

1. Slowly squeeze a small amount of UV resin into the teardrop mold, filling it about halfway (**A**).

2. Using tweezers, add one to three pieces of purple and white baby's breath flowers and three to five baby's breath flower buds (**B**).

3. Drop in a few pieces of silver gravel for added texture and arrange the pattern using a plastic rod or toothpick (**C**).

4. Cure under a UV lamp for 2 minutes. Then, add more UV resin to fill the mold to the top – there's no need to create a dome at this stage as the back will be built up later.

5. Cure again for 2 minutes and carefully demold the pendant (**D**).

6. Flip the pendant over and apply a thin layer of UV resin to the back.

7. Using a plastic rod or tweezers, add blue metal foil shavings to create a mosaic pattern (**E**). Cure under UV light for 2 minutes.

8. Brush a layer of black gel nail polish evenly across the surface (**F**). Cure for another 2 minutes.

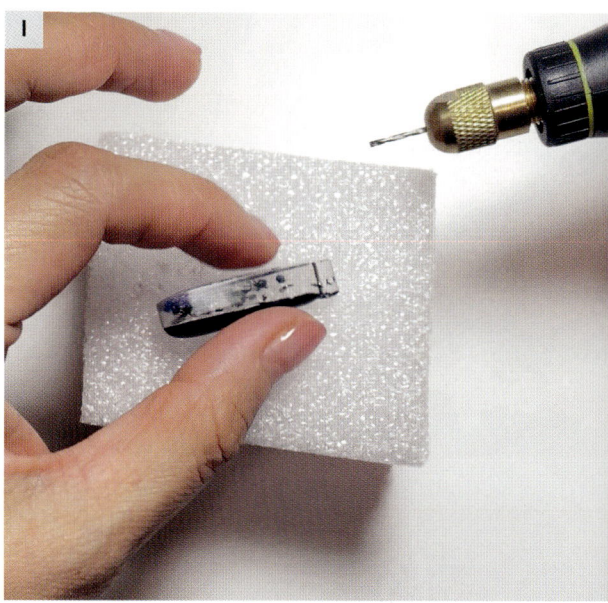

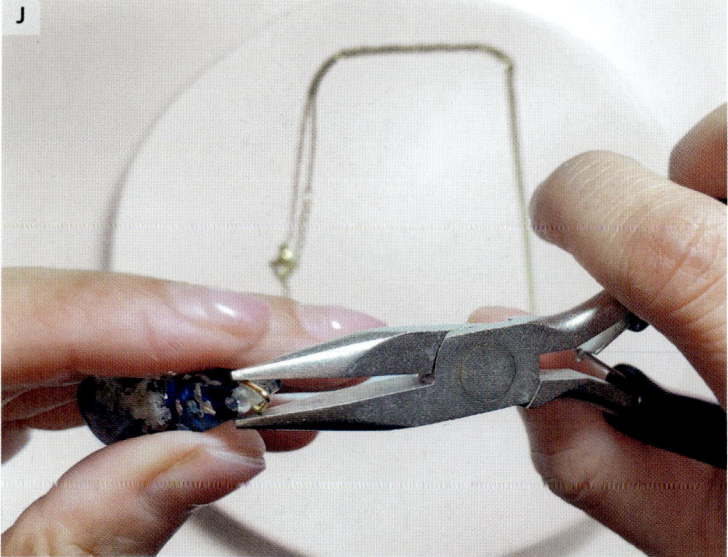

9. Apply a final coating of UV resin (**G**). Cure for 2 minutes to seal the design.

10. Apply a final layer of UV resin to the front of the pendant to create a dome (**H**).

11. Place on a stiff foam block or cushion and use a handheld jewelry drill to make a small hole near the top tip of the pendant (**I**). Brush off any excess dust using a powder brush.

12. Insert a jump ring through the hole using jewelry pliers (**J**).

13. Attach the necklace chain to complete the piece.

Project 31:

Cypress earrings

Cypress leaves are another abundant and versatile botanical element. Their rich dark-green color naturally evokes the feeling of winter, while their shape can be easily trimmed into different sizes without losing character. In this design, the focus is on accenting the pendant: the bottom half is layered with cypress leaves, while silver glitter fills the upper space. The result is a piece that feels both earthy and radiant – perfectly balancing natural texture with a touch of sparkle.

You will need

- ❀ Silicone mold with olive shape and built-in through hole
- ❀ UV resin
- ❀ Plastic rod or toothpick
- ❀ Tweezers
- ❀ Pressed cypress leaves
- ❀ Silver glitter powder
- ❀ UV lamp
- ❀ Jewelry pliers (flat nose)
- ❀ Jewelry findings (two ear hooks, two 0.7 x 6mm jump rings all in sterling silver)

1. Slowly squeeze a small amount of UV resin into the olive-shaped mold to about half of its depth (**A**).

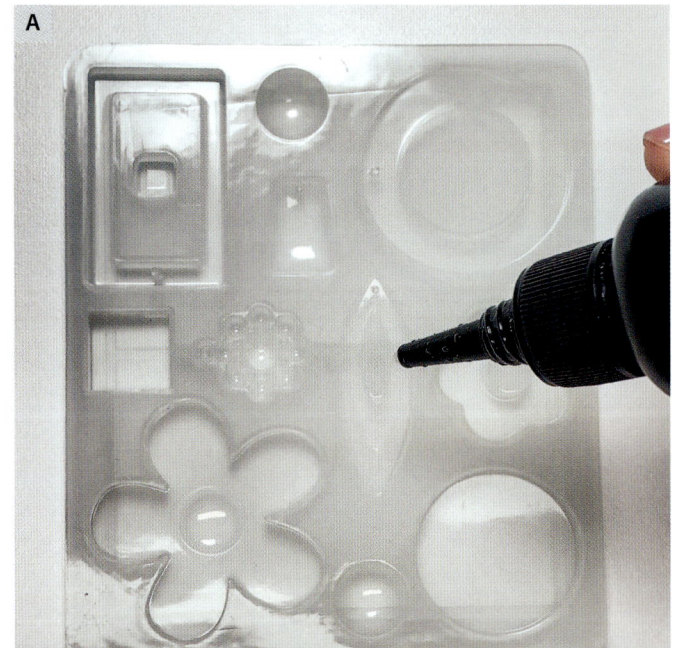

A

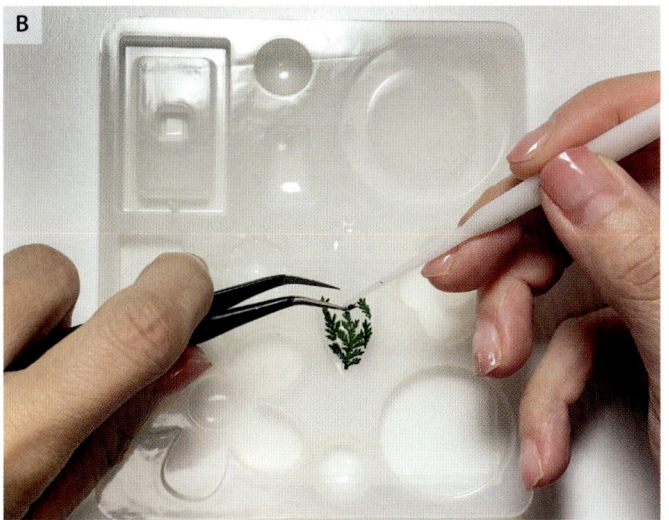

2. Using tweezers, add four to five pieces of cypress leaf, trimmed to smaller sizes, arranging them to cover the bottom third of the mold (**B**). Use a plastic rod to remove any air bubbles.

3. Apply a small amount of UV resin to the tip of a plastic stick, dip it into silver glitter powder (**C**), and gently distribute the glitter into the top two-thirds of the resin. Cure the piece under a UV lamp for 2 minutes.

4. Add more UV resin to fill the mold completely, allowing for a slight dome at the top (**D**).

5. Cure under UV light again for 2 minutes, then carefully demold the pendant. Repeat to make a second pendant.

6. Since the mold includes a built-in hole, there is no need to drill. Simply insert a jump ring through each hole using jewelry pliers (**E**).

7. Attach an ear hook to each jump ring to complete the earrings (**F**).

Project 32:

Purple statice and blue cornflower large earrings

This design is a variation on the blue and green baby's breath earrings but with a bolder color story and layered effects. The earrings are crafted using a round mold for the stud and a rainbow-arch mold for the dangling pendant. For the studs, only blue and purple flowers were used to create a clean, vibrant contrast. The pendants, however, incorporate gold foil shapes alongside the purple statice and blue cornflower, adding richness and a layered, multidimensional look. The two parts are connected with a delicate gold chain, which can be customized in length. A shorter chain brings the pendant closer to the stud, emphasizing the floral and foil details in a tighter composition, while a longer chain gives the earrings a graceful, dangling effect that highlights their movement and sparkle.

You will need

- Silicone mold with small circular button shape (⅝–¾in (15–20mm) in diameter)
- UV resin
- Tweezers
- Air-dried purple statice and blue cornflower flowers
- Gold foil shavings
- Plastic rod or toothpick
- UV lamp

- Silicone mold with large arch shape (1½in (40mm))
- Handheld UV pen
- Alcohol or mild soap
- Jewelry pliers (flat nose)
- Jewelry findings (loose cable chain cut to 1in (25mm), two 4mm flat pad earrings posts, two 5mm triangle jump rings, two 0.7 x 5mm jump rings all in gold-plated stainless steel)

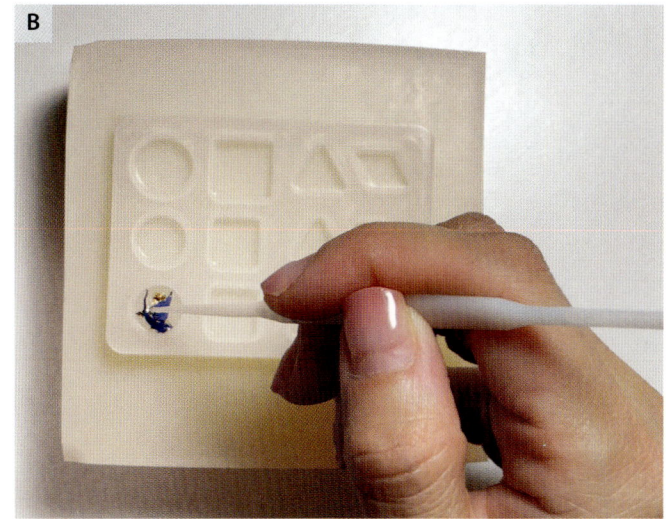

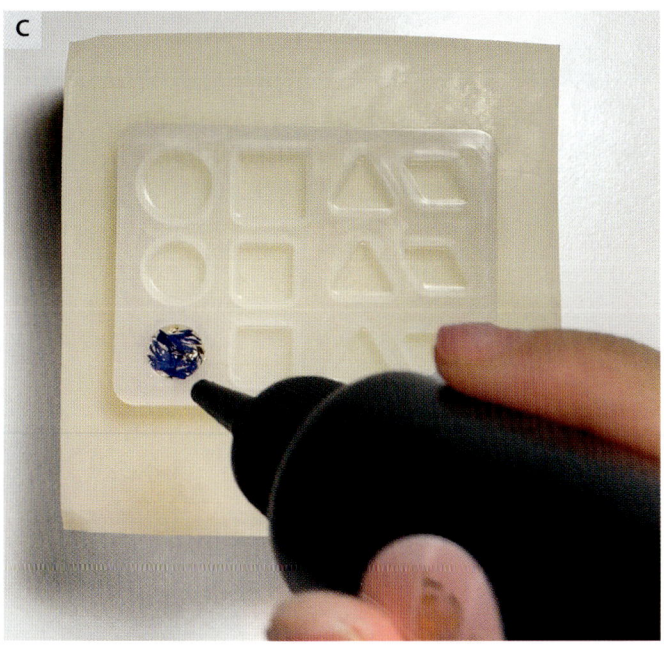

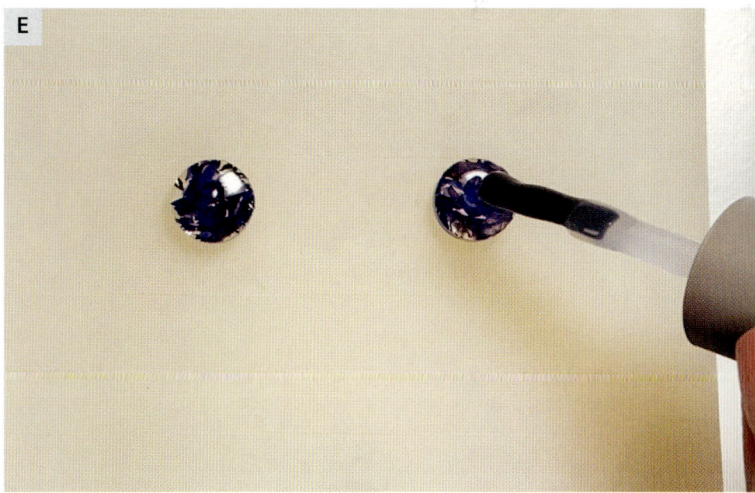

1. To make the resin stud, slowly apply a thin layer of UV resin into the button mold (**A**).

2. Use tweezers or a plastic rod to add blue cornflowers and a small amount of gold foil shavings (**B**).

3. Then, add more UV resin to fill the mold completely and form a slight dome (**C**).

4. Cure under UV light for 2 minutes. Once cured, demold the piece carefully. Repeat to make a second pendant. (**D**).

5. Apply a thin dome layer of UV resin to the front of the pendant to create a glossy finish and a slight dome (**E**). Cure it under the UV lamp for 2 minutes once more.

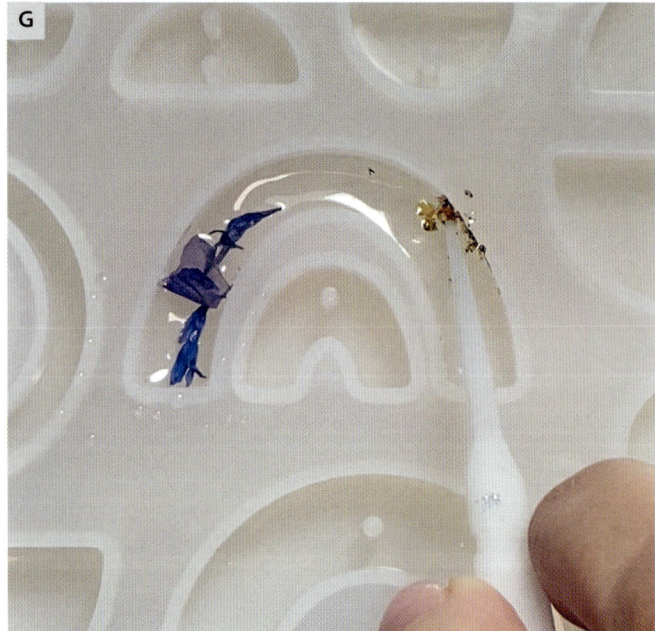

6. Clean the flat pad earring post with alcohol or mild soap to remove oils or dust. Use a drop of UV resin to glue the post to the center back of the stud (F). Cure it under UV light for 2 minutes.

7. To make the pendant, slowly squeeze a small amount of UV resin into the large arch mold, filling it about halfway. Arrange purple statice and blue cornflowers into the resin, using tweezers for precision, and fill the spaces with gold foil shavings (G). Remember, the bottom of the mold will become the front of the pendant.

8. Cure under a UV lamp for 2 minutes. Then, apply another layer of UV resin to fill the mold completely (H), and cure again.

9. Once cured, demold the piece carefully. Apply a thin dome layer of UV resin to the front of the pendant to create a glossy finish and a slight dome (I) and cure it under the UV light.

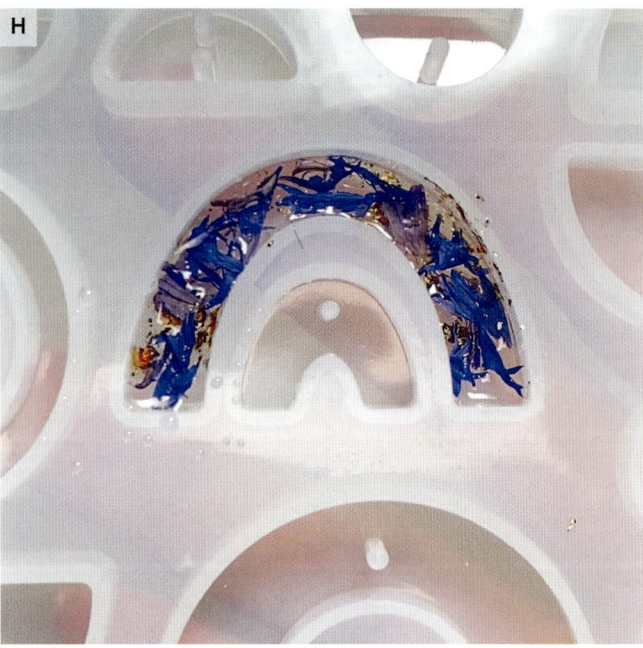

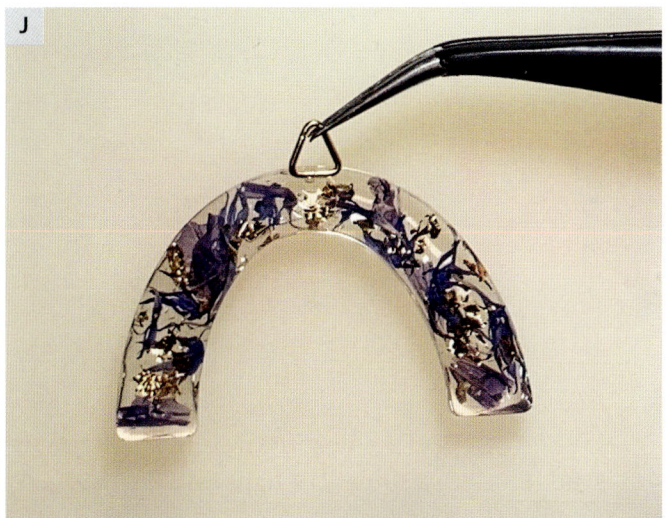

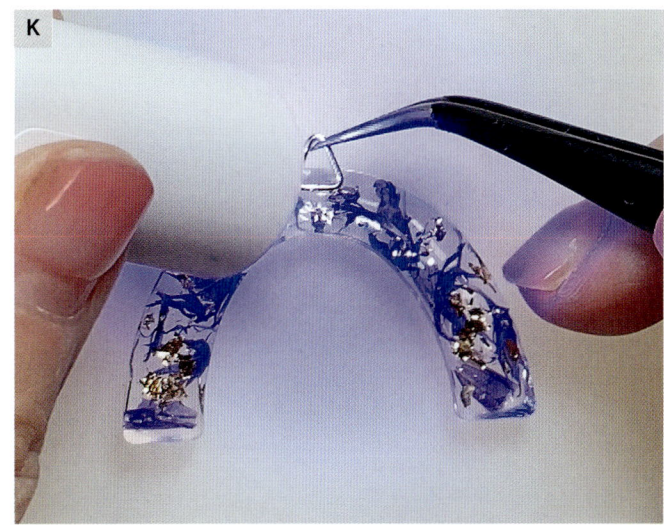

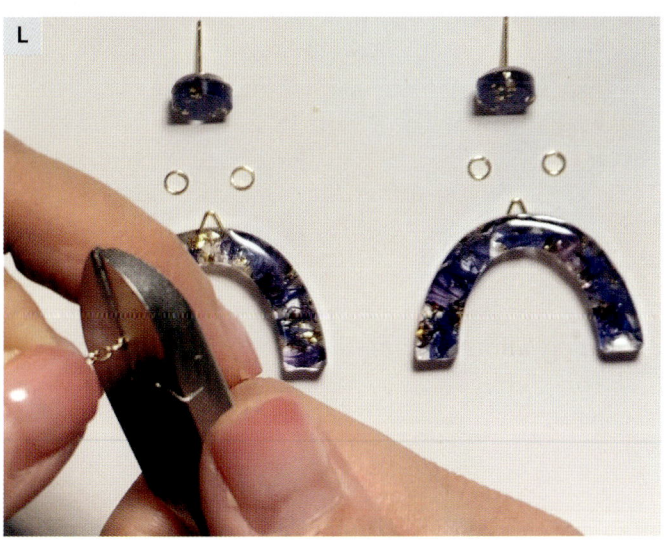

10. Place the pendant facing up on the silicone block. Use pliers to glue a triangle jump ring on the top of the arch (J).

11. Cure under a handheld UV pen for 1 minute (K). Repeat to make a second pendant.

12. Cut loose cable chain to about ¾in (1.5cm) using cutting pliers (L). Fold the chain in half and thread the folded end through the triangle jump ring on each pendant.

13. Using a jump ring, connect both ends of the folded chain to the ring on the stud earring. Close the jump rings securely to complete the earrings (M).

Project 33:

Christmas earrings

These earrings feature a petite gem-shaped stud paired with a dainty freshwater pearl that dangles gracefully beneath. Inspired by the classic palette of the season – red, green, and gold – the design combines natural and decorative elements: a red rosary pea (love bean) for the vibrant red, a small cypress leaf for fresh green, and shimmering gold gravel for the golden accents. Arranged carefully within the gem mold, the composition captures the warmth and cheer of Christmas. The addition of the pearl brings a touch of luxury and softness, making the earrings both festive and elegant.

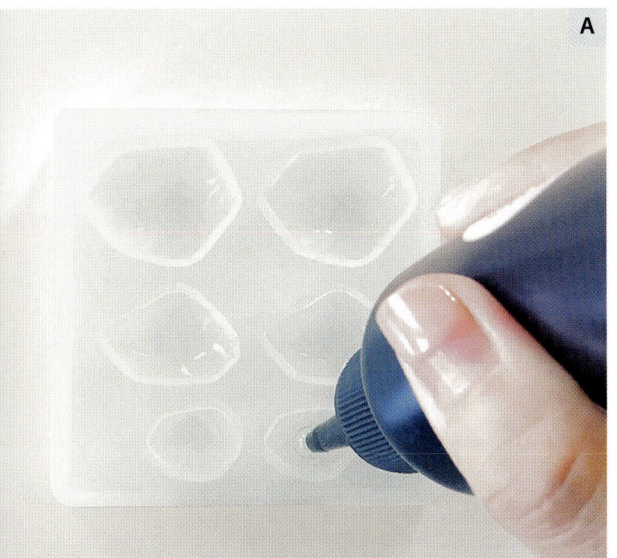

You will need

- ❖ Silicone mold with small irregular stone shape
- ❖ UV resin
- ❖ Gold gravel
- ❖ Plastic rod or toothpick
- ❖ Tweezers
- ❖ Dried rosary pea
- ❖ Pressed cypress leaves
- ❖ UV lamp
- ❖ Silicone block
- ❖ Alcohol or mild soap
- ❖ Handheld UV pen
- ❖ Jewelry pliers (flat nose)
- ❖ Jewelry findings (two flat pad earring posts, two 0.7 x 6mm jump rings all in gold-plated stainless steel)
- ❖ Two 4mm freshwater pearl pendants

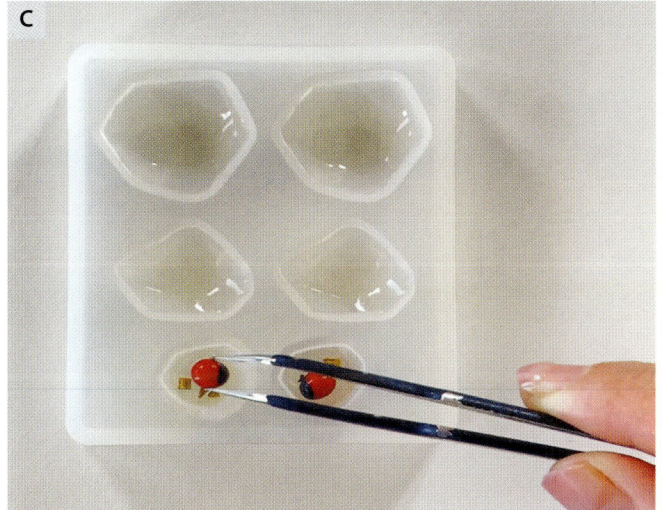

1. Slowly squeeze just one to two drops of UV resin into two molds, filling them to about one-third of their depth (A).

2. Place a few pieces of gold gravel into the resin using a plastic rod or toothpick (B).

3. Add a single rosary pea and a few tiny fragments of cypress leaf to each mold, using tweezers (C). Cure this initial layer under a UV lamp for 2 minutes.

4. Next, apply another layer of UV resin to bring the fill level to about two-thirds (D).

5. Use tweezers to add a slightly larger piece of cypress leaf to each pendant for visual depth and contrast (E). Cure under the UV lamp for another 2 minutes.

6. Finally, fill each mold completely with UV resin and create a gentle dome at the surface. Cure this final layer under the UV lamp for two minutes.

7. Clean the flat pad earring posts with alcohol or mild soap to remove any oils or dust.

8. Carefully demold the cured earring studs and place them on the silicone block. Use a drop of UV resin to glue the flat pad posts onto the center back of each stud (F). Cure under UV light for 2 minutes.

9. Use jump rings to connect the pearl pendants with the rings on the earring posts (G).

Conclusion

As we close this creative journey, I hope you feel both inspired and equipped to make resin jewelry that expresses your creativity in a sustainable and meaningful way. This journey is more than learning how to pour, cure, and polish. It's about pausing to appreciate the delicate curve of a petal, the quiet transformation of resin into form, and the thoughtful choices that support an eco-friendlier, plant-based, and sustainable lifestyle.

Every flower you press, every botanical you preserve, and every mindful material you choose brings us one step closer to a more sustainable lifestyle rooted in intention and responsibility.

Resin jewelry has the power to tell stories – of seasons, of emotions, of transformation, and now, also of environmental awareness. Let your creations reflect not only your artistic voice but also your commitment to a greener, kinder world.

As you continue crafting, may your hands stay curious, your heart stay rooted, and your art speak gently but powerfully of the world you want to build.

Suppliers

Plant-based/eco-friendly UV resin

Brand	Country/region	Plant source	Website
Anycubic ECO Resin	China/global	Soybean oil	anycubic.com
Elegoo Plant-Based Resin	USA/global	Soy-based photopolymer	us.elegoo.com
Esun eResin-PLA Pro	China/global	PLA (corn-derived)	esun3d.com
Green Stuff World	Spain/EU	Eco-formulated	greenstuffworld.com

Plant-based epoxy resin

Brand	Country/region	Bio-based content	Plant source	Website
Crestapol® 1260 Bio	UK	25–35%	Plant-based polyols	scottbader.com
EcoPoxy®	Canada/global	Up to 70%	Soy, cashew shell oil	ecopoxy.com
Entropy Resins®	USA/global	Up to 50%	Pine oil, plant oils	entropyresins.com
GlassCast® Eco	UK/EU	30–40%	Plant oils	glasscastresin.com
GreenPoxy® (Sicomin)	France/EU	33–55%	Vegetable oils	sicomin.com
Gurit AMPRO® Bio	Switzerland/global	~35%	Vegetable oils	gurit.com

Plant-based and vegan nail polish

Brand	Country/region	Plant-based content	Website
BKIND	Canada	77%	bkind.com
Manucurist	France/global	Up to 84%	us.manucurist.com
Nailtopia	USA	85% bio-sourced	nailtopia.com
Nails.INC®	UK/global	73%	nailsinc.com
Sienna™ Byron Bay	Australia	100% sugarcane, cassava	sienna.co

Eco jewelry tools, findings, eco glitters and pigments

Category	Brand/supplier	Country	Website/link	Eco/ethical highlights
Eco jewelry tools	Otto Frei	USA / Global	ottofrei.com	Family-run, some eco-friendly tools
Eco jewelry tools	Halstead™	USA	halsteadbead.com	Recycled silver, sustainability efforts
Jewelry findings	Kiwa Seisakujo	Japan	kiwaseisakujo.jp/en	Handmade parts and accessories
Jewelry findings	Rio Grande	USA	riogrande.com	Recycled metals available
Eco jewelry findings	Eco Findings (Etsy)	UK	etsy.com/shop/ecofindings	Recycled metals, handcrafted
Eco glitter	Bioglitter® by Today Glitter	USA	todayglitter.com	Biodegradable cosmetic-grade
Eco pigments	Earth Pigments	USA	earthpigments.com	Natural mineral pigments
Eco pigments	Natural Earth Paint	USA	naturalearthpaint.com	Natural, non-toxic pigments

Acknowledgments

This book would not have been possible without the love and support of my family.

To my husband – who not only stood beside me but also became the photographer and picture editor for this project – your patience, creativity, and encouragement brought so much beauty to these pages

To my daughters, your cheerful spirits brighten my days and remind me of the joy in small things. I have enjoyed your company in the process of growing, picking, and preserving flowers, making this journey all the more meaningful. Thank you for inspiring me in ways you may not even realize.

Special thanks to Jingxuan and Sasha (overleaf), whose grace and presence as photo models brought the images in this book to life.

I am also grateful to my dear sister and my friends Huilin and Cici, who cheered me on and helped me stay on track throughout the writing process.

My appreciation also goes to the endless inspiration found in the flowers themselves.

To everyone who supported me, in both big and small ways, please know this book carries pieces of you within it.

Glossary

A

Alcohol ink: A fast-drying, dye-based ink used to color resin and create marbling or abstract effects.

B

Bail: A jewelry finding that connects a pendant to a chain or cord.

Bezel: A flat-backed frame, often with walls, that holds resin and decorative elements.

C

Chain-nose pliers: Tapered pliers used for opening and closing jump rings or gripping wire.

Clasp: A closure mechanism used to fasten necklaces or bracelets; common types include lobster, toggle, magnetic, and spring ring.

Colorant: Pigments, mica powders, or dyes used to tint resin.

Connector: A component with multiple loops used to join different parts of a jewelry piece.

Curing: The chemical reaction that turns liquid resin into a hardened solid form.

Cure time: The duration required for resin to fully harden/set.

D

Desiccant: A drying agent (e.g., silica gel) used to preserve flowers or absorb moisture from environments.

Dome: A slightly raised, rounded resin surface created by overfilling a mold or bezel.

E

Earring hook (fishhook): A wire finding that loops through a pierced ear and supports a resin dangle.

Epoxy resin: A two-part resin system that cures at room temperature and is ideal for jewelry and small castings.

Eye pin: A straight wire with a loop at one end, used to hold beads or resin charms.

F

Findings: The collective term for all metal components used to assemble jewelry (e.g., clasps, bails, rings, pins).

Flat-nose pliers: Jewelry pliers with flat, rectangular jaws, used for gripping or holding flat components.

H

Hardener: The component that reacts with resin to initiate the curing process in epoxy systems.

Headpin: A straight wire with a flat or decorative end, used to string beads or resin elements.

I

Inclusion: Any object embedded within resin, such as dried flowers, glitter, foil, or beads.

J

Jewelry drill: A small handheld tool used to drill holes into cured resin pieces.

Jewelry wire: Wire used to create structure or string elements in jewelry making. Comes in various gauges.

Jump ring: A metal ring used to connect components; available as open or closed.

L

Layering: A technique in resin pouring where different layers are added and cured in stages to create depth.

Leather cord: A natural or faux leather strip used in bohemian or rustic jewelry designs.

Lobster clasp: A popular clasp shaped like a lobster claw with a spring-loaded gate.

M

Mica powder: A shimmering powdered pigment often added to resin for a pearlescent effect.

Mixing cup: A container used to measure and combine resin and hardener.

Mixing ratio: The specific proportion of resin to hardener as recommended by the manufacturer.

Mold: A flexible silicone or plastic cavity into which resin is poured and shaped.

P

Pendant frame: A bezel or open metal frame used as a base for resin or pressed-flower pendants.

Pigment: A substance used to color resin; may be powdered, liquid, or paste form.

Pinch bail: A type of bail that snaps into a drilled hole in a pendant without glue.

Pressed flower: A dried flower flattened using a press or book for embedding in resin.

Pot life: The amount of working time you have before the resin starts to cure and harden.

R

Resin: A synthetic liquid that cures into a hard, clear, or colored plastic-like material.

Round-nose pliers: Pliers with rounded jaws used to make loops in wire.

S

Sanding: The process of smoothing or finishing resin surfaces using sandpaper or polishing tools.

Silicone block: A reusable, non-stick work surface ideal for resin work.

Silicone mold: A flexible mold made from silicone rubber used for casting resin shapes.

Split ring: A tightly wound double-loop ring used as a secure alternative to jump rings.

Spring ring clasp: A round clasp that opens with a spring mechanism.

T

Tack-free time: The amount of time it takes for the resin surface to no longer feel sticky.

Torch: A small butane torch used to remove bubbles from the resin surface.

Topcoat: A clear layer of resin applied to a piece to restore or enhance gloss.

U

UV lamp: A light source used to cure ultraviolet (UV) resin quickly.

UV resin: A single-part resin that cures under UV light, ideal for small, quick projects.

W

Working life: The time you can take to use resin (coating, casting etc.) before it starts to get hard.